'Austen Hardwick loves Jesus,
kind of captivating, free-flowin
read. So, if you're interested in
if you're not at this moment – yc
book. It will make you want to o_ _ _ _ _____ to God and put
on your running shoes. "My faith feels . . . on the move", he
writes. "It has been tried and tested, rebounded and informed,
and it feels more alive than ever before." I want to run alongside a man who can truthfully say that. I think you will, too, by
the time you've read the first couple of pages.'

Chick Yuill, writer, speaker and runner

'I have known Austen for a long time but have never run with
him, mainly because I couldn't keep up. However, all who
read this text will finish the book feeling like they have jogged
alongside him listening to his story, finding so many echoes of
their own life in his. My midlife crisis was endurance events,
and any of us who have hit "the wall" and run through it in life
or on the road will resonate with much of what Austen writes.
This is not a "Chariots of Fire" book with a Hollywood ending;
rather, it is a book about running and a book about a life of suffering, doubt, fear, faith and love. It is real, earthy and relevant
in a powerful way, and because of this it is a "deep" book which
will both move and inspire.'

Phil Wall, leadership coach

'Moving, honest, vulnerable, challenging and, above all, inspirational. Written in a wonderfully accessible way, here is wisdom to help us finish the really big race.'

Rob Parsons, Founder and Chairman, Care for the Family

'As a neurosurgeon I have the unique privilege of "looking" into my patients' brains. I am very rarely allowed to "see" their souls. Through Austen's book I was afforded this rare opportunity. It is a remarkable achievement from a deeply religious but very modern man. If you are a Christian, you will be part of an amazing journey that will challenge you but also reinforce your belief. If you are not, this is a rare opportunity to understand and appreciate the common struggles of faith, hope and love. Austen is a very focused "runner". Reading his thoughts, I saw myself focusing in my surgery to the exclusion of almost everything around me. This is a profound religious experience and this book will let you share in it.'

Christos Tolias, Consultant Neurosurgeon, Clinical Lead Neurosurgery, Kings College Hospital, London

'In this highly autobiographical book, three-time stroke survivor Austen Hardwick writes honestly about his experience of running and believing. Thoughtful and challenging, *Ever Present* describes with vulnerability some of the joys and frustrations of following Christ in the race of life.'

Matthew Porter, Vicar, The Belfrey, York, and author

Ever Present

Running to survive, thrive and believe

Austen Hardwick

Authentic

First published 2020 by Authentic Media Limited,
PO Box 6326, Bletchley, Milton Keynes, MK1 9GG.
authenticmedia.co.uk

British Library Cataloguing in Publication Data
A catalogue record for this book is available from the British Library.
ISBN: 978-1-78893-136-6
978-1-78893-137-3 (e-book)

Cover design by Mercedes Piñera
Printed and bound by CPI Group (UK) Ltd, Croydon, CR0 4YY

Contents

To my wife Helen – selfless and ever present through it all.

Acknowledgements

I am grateful to the friends who have travelled with me, especially Gordon and Jonny, for your wisdom and humour in helping me forwards. Not forgetting Matt for the music and bond of friendship born at Mount Crags to this day (YDB). To Thomas, Don and Anthony; for unexpected coffees and encouragement. Likewise to Fin Macrae for bridging the 660 miles with so much common ground.

To the humble powerhouse of Tadcaster's St Mary's Church, Peter Hodgson, and his insightful wife Fay; for always challenging me over 'beetroot at twelve'.

To Rob Parsons and Chick Yuill; for your advice to a new author. Equally, to the team at Authentic Media for valuing my story; special thanks to Donna, Rachael, Becky and Charlie for your expertise and direction.

To Christos Tolias, MD, PhD, FRCS(Engl), FRCS(SN), Consultant Neurosurgeon, Lead Clinician Neurosurgery at King's College Hospital; and the heroes of our NHS, faultless in their care.

Finally, this book would not have been possible without the input of experienced runners. My sincere appreciation to Ian Richards (OLY) for your openness and shared belief that God's pleasure can be felt when we are fast. Thank you to Edwin; your humility and service to our town is exemplary, and to William (Bill) O'Connor, a real 'Ever Present' marathon runner, for your hospitality and inspiring approach to challenge. May our running friendship go the full 26.2 miles.

Foreword

Eric Liddell of *Chariots of Fire* fame is quoted as saying *'God . . . made me fast. And when I run, I feel His pleasure.'* By contrast, in this book *Ever Present*, marathon runner Austen Hardwick implies that *when he runs, he feels God's presence.* It is as though, for Liddell, God was present in his life but more as a spectator when he was running. Austen describes God as always being there on his shoulder, going through all that life throws at him, but when he runs, he feels especially close. And Austen has had some pretty tough stuff to deal with.

When I first started to read the book, I was so captivated that I wanted to rush through to the finish to discover what happens but then, as an Olympian, my mindset is to always press on towards the goal as quickly as possible. However, the more I read, the more I had to stop to think. There are so many challenges to my way of thinking in this book. The biggest being, have I been missing out? One of the key criteria to moving fast is the efficiency of how you use your body, with elite athletes constantly looking for minor adjustments. The theory is simple: many marginal gains can make a significant difference. *Ever Present*, however, has made me give much consideration to the gains that could come from the harmonisation of mind, body and spirit, which Austen has clearly found, not only for the benefit of my sporting performance but life in general. This book is very much about exploring the relationship between running and believing which is quite unique and not the more usual story of how God/Jesus has helped a sportsman excel, often overcoming adversity along the way.

Austen is an artist who is not only able to paint but is also able to draw word pictures about situations and the environment in which he has found himself that instantly capture your attention. For example, having a stroke would be worrying for anyone, but having three takes you to a place where every aspect of your life is under serious threat. Yet Austen is able to bring readers close to his predicament by talking about the old speaking clock and those all-too-familiar words 'at the third stroke it will be . . .'. Analogies such as this abound in the book and make it a joy to read.

This is certainly a book that I shall be reading many times over and will be keeping on my bookshelf for future reference.

Ian Richards OLY
1980 Olympian and currently one of the world's top masters athletes having won 8 world age group championships and set 6 world age records in the last 10 years

Introduction:
Finding the Blue Line

If you want acquaintances, tell them your successes. If you want friends, tell them your fears.[1]

I have never written a book before, but until five years ago I had never suffered a stroke, experienced epileptic seizures or confronted brain surgery either. Sure, my life has had plenty of variety; I've enjoyed fifteen years as a teacher in primary education, I've trained and served as a minister of religion for nine years, met a wonderful woman in 1994 who became my wife and with whom we do our best, like many others, at parenting on instinct twenty-six years later. I've also discovered joy in running and a fascination with God.

After the trauma of the initial diagnosis of my brain condition, a cavernous malformation (or cavernoma[2]), I needed to find out more from the experts. I travelled to London and nearly fell off my chair high up in the lecture theatre of the Queen Square Institute of Neurology as a professor highlighted the chances of brain haemorrhage for those in their forties, particularly working in stressful occupations such as education; I fitted his data so well.[3]

Medical events force their way into life as uninvited guests, crashing onto our shores as life-changing waves before retreating to leave us pregnant with experience. Since my first stroke, such events had become a too-familiar part of my life, so I decided to do something with the debris of thoughts and started my first writing project, one week after I returned home from a second attempt at neurosurgery.

The challenge of writing a book felt as mountainous as the schedule when I commenced proper training for my first London Marathon. That sounds boastful; the truth is, I have only run two marathons – but two are enough to testify to the pressure that a man with a long-term project places upon a family. Had I truly thought this through? The hours of dedication, the consuming physical and mental commitment, the dwindling variety to my conversation, the lack of sleep, the risk that I may not even complete it?

That first marathon run was in April 1998 when I was given the opportunity to represent the Bobby Moore Fund for Cancer Research UK.[4] I was carefree, engaged to my wife and out training when I should probably have been writing wedding invitations. But the truth is, with marathon training, there is always something else that you could be doing. We choose how to spend our time, it is limited, and I don't think there is ever a convenient season to begin a project that involves three or four evenings a week over a six-month period. But there I was on my first marathon eve, at the end of half a year of plate-spinning – thanks to a fiancée of immense patience – and with a stomach full of pasta.

I woke on marathon morning and walked my normal route across the landing to the bathroom, so familiar in the east London terraced house in which I had grown up. Adrenaline was already running through me and I was a little confused to notice a broken blue line marking my way along the carpet. For serious marathoners, the broken blue line painted onto the road marks the shortest possible route around London's iconic course. Following this provides opportunity for faster times and it is officially painted three days before the race with a quick-drying and easily removable substance called Tempro. Generally, the race is so crowded that pavement plodders like me hardly get to see the blue line as we weave in and out of fancy-dress rhinos and superheroes, until the field spreads out towards the agonising latter stages of the race or after three hours of running. With a humorous nod to this ordeal that lay ahead, my parents had decided to mark my course from bedroom to bathroom to kitchen to front door with a line of chopped blue electrical tape. I've always appreciated subtlety. There followed breakfast, kit checks, into the car and a final hug beneath a Blackheath sunrise, before I headed off to find the real blue line.

Twenty years later and on the December morning when I began writing, once again a clear blue sky welcomed the perfect sunrise; as a qualified art teacher I knew that orange and navy were complementary colours and it is striking how often nature presents them as neighbours. Christmas was almost here. The red-brick town houses around our estate glowed a warm terracotta, like a hill of opened Nike shoeboxes. Elbowing tree branches resembled shapes of crisps in bowls of Advent hospitality and leaf edges sparkled like razor-sharp glass in the wintry honesty of daylight. The clarity afforded by such weather was appropriate because gazing out of the window at the top of Singleton Hill, where we lived, I resolved to begin an honest project; one which would allow you and I to see more clearly.

This book is not one of those self-help fitness or wellbeing manuals where I get into your head with strategies which make you pumped on life. Instead I have shared weakness. I especially set out to cut through the haze of religious baggage or assumed understanding that those of us with a history within church seem to accumulate. It felt like gliding a pair of scissors through an old garment, the blades of which came to represent two things that are dear to me; how it feels to run (to communicate the joy running brings me and the frustrations that come with it) and what this mix of discipline and endurance has taught me about being a Christian. I find the two to be inseparable since I became a regular runner, but what I did not anticipate was the new light they could shed upon each other, like parables being written each time I lace up to go running.

Jesus painted pictures upon his listeners' minds that made them go away and think. His parables were uncomfortable and challenged prejudice, pride and fear. I have also found that it is not my successes, so much as my discomforts, my fears, that I return to most when exercising and thinking about God. I have run sporadically most of my life, more deliberately so during the last twenty years; I've walked with God for slightly longer. Both these relationships have been loud and deliberate; at other times, reluctant and fearful. There have been the celebrations, the wall of sound and high-fives of London's Tower Bridge crowds, but equally there have been the lows of a silent Blackfriars Underpass and the tantrums and mental anguish of hitting the dreaded runner's wall. My Christian faith has also seen both headlines and small print – the miracles of healing but equally the confusion and pain of unanswered prayers, and I'm left wondering if God has a blue line at all, a reliable route through this paradox? I have even considered the easier option of abandoning my search for his way, the Tempro for this marathon of living, but I have stuck around and believe that running has a lot to do with it.

But let me say from the starting line that I'm not interested in a simple path to follow, nor an easy, obvious route; I'm grateful for my freedom to make choices and with it, to make mistakes. Like a runner desperate for carbohydrates, protein or a recovery drink, what I crave most these days is God and to find the blue line consisting of himself; his revealed character and my experience of it, which I believe will be sufficient for my tired legs. I propose in this book that knowing him is more important than hitching a ride using someone else's map, believing in a denomination's prescribed path or succumbing to neat clichés which paper over the cracks.

This God-life is about choices; audaciously open-ended, a knife-edge of liberation with parameters, abandonment, but still being known. We run a race and sometimes the road ahead that we have chosen looks tougher than we were prepared for by those that believe. At its worst and best, we just have to admit that we are lost, the satellite signal on our wrist has vanished and we are finally bankrupt of any intellectual argument or acquired wisdom. Then, and only then, can recovery commence.

This book about running and faith often refers to art, another of my loves. I dabbled my brush in the Renaissance at A level and later at art college, learning enough about symbolism of colour to know that Mary, often depicted in dazzling blue garments, symbolised purity as her expensive lapis lazuli pigment often took centre stage within work designed both to worship and educate. Of course, the precious marathon Tempro line just had to be blue.

But there is another art which I have neglected along the way, that of taking in enough refreshment to sustain the rhythm of my spiritual life. Running is a sport of balances, and I have often fallen into the trap of losing God's blue line when

I have not drunk in enough, pressing pause, as you will see from my own story. James Fixx taught that hydration becomes a deliberate and conscious artform for serious runners and I hope this book encourages you to take refreshment before you feel thirsty.[5]

My race, probably like yours, has been peppered with fears: health, wealth, relationships, relatives, leadership, being a follower – the list goes on, and the sleepless nights have held many secrets. But out of all this, I have decided to stick with God and to run towards instead of away from him for one simple reason: I once read that he came for the thirsty and the lost ones, like me and like you.

I wonder what stares back at you in the morning mirror? Do you squint at your silhouette? Does your dehydrated skin tell the stories of miles already covered? You may well be part of our Fitbit generation, obsessed with calories, steps, heartbeats and winning at life from the self-censored social media footprint you crave to purport. Yet you will soon see that this book is not about winning. My marathon running (an obsession still in its infancy, I hope) has been an epiphany in taking part shoulder to shoulder with acquaintances who have become friends. In this book, I delve into this distance; why watching it and taking part in it have made such an impression upon me as a follower of Christ. The 1981 London Marathon had 7055 starters lining up at Greenwich with 7055 unique stories to tell, but the essential point for me is that very few of them were there to *win* the race. Running in its various forms has seen an explosion during the last decade and many people have talked to me about its impact, not just in health terms but in the emotional and spiritual realms, so when it comes to running a marathon, look no further for the greatest leveller parable you may possibly ever know.

You might be a shadow of your past best-self, struggling with the frustration of injury or, like me five years ago, unable to walk without a Zimmer frame until your post-haemorrhage leg awoke. The chances are that you will be somewhere along the scale from the form of your life to one which has regrettably slipped from 5k to couch, and I want to help you in the only way I currently know; by seeking God's blue line. So, here is a book about the joys and frustrations of running and the discipline and endurance needed to remain a Christian; my honest conversation between running and believing.

I therefore invite you to become a friend, and as we say at Parkrun every Saturday morning, 'Let's go running!'

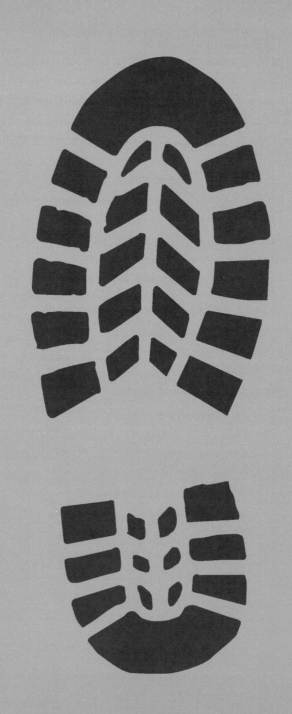

1

At the Third Stroke

And now these three remain: faith, hope and love. But the greatest of these is love.[1]

I've attended enough weddings to know that these words of the apostle Paul written to the early church can be a cliché of many ceremonies. They follow a projection of what husband and wife hope to become as they embark upon their lives as loving spouses; patient, forgiving, truthful – it's a list of virtues I achieve when I'm in a good mood but not when the washing-up needs doing or the family are screaming about time allocation in the bathroom. Everybody approves in the soft-focus atmosphere of the crumbling church walls, as sweaty palms cling to orders of service and we leave feeling like all conscience boxes are freshly ticked when it comes to loving our other halves.

These words came back to me in a completely new way as I lay helpless in a hospital bed in November 2017, my palm clinging to the glossy revamped hospital menu. After a third brain haemorrhage in just beyond as many years, and consequently my third stroke, I began to see that faith, hope and love represented three experiences which had become the corners of a triangle during my life: faith was my Christian experience as somebody with a changing understanding of what 'fullness of life'[2] might mean, hope had always accompanied my experience of sickness like a surprising parrot permanently perched upon this woeful voyager's shoulder, and love encapsulated my experience of freedom through running. When I say 'love', it is because I invest time in it, diary it, and it holds a reciprocal life-affirming quality which brings me to a more mentally and physically healthy place in my own self. In this book, fullness of life, suffering and running are therefore representative, on one level, of what I mean when I speak of faith, hope and love.

There is an irony to having three strokes, as a piece of British cultural history flew into my hospital patient mind as a person with a weakness for words. It seems impossible in our personalised, device-saturated age, but the Speaking Clock first spoke in 1936 with the voice of Ethel Jane Cain, a Post Office exchange operator from Croydon. Since then, 'At the third stroke' is a cultural quirk which has traditionally been the opening words of the voiced British dial-the-time service which at its peak had millions dialling 123 each year to hear an accurate time. Sometimes genuinely sought, at other times to combat loneliness, the voice and words were reassuring and consistent, much like the wedding words of Paul. As a runner with a Christian faith but further from being a serious theologian than Blackheath is to The Mall, I had long been considering a book about the impact of running upon what I believe and vice versa, and this third stroke was the right time; a moment of decision when the clock spoke. I didn't hear a voice from God, I never have – but I resolved to make use of the unplanned time-out as an opportunity to bring some strands from my life of running and believing together, using faith, hope and love as the three markers on our course.

First some personal history. Born in 1974, I am old enough to appreciate Commodore as a retro computer brand and would happily Dad-dance in a Subbuteo T-shirt. Stepping back around thirty-five years, I grew up in that age of early video-gaming with a console the size of a small suitcase, when one of the earliest arcade games had two thin lines (or pixelated rackets) which could be height-adjusted using a wheel on a controller to make a small square ball rebound back and forth across the screen. This clumsy game of table tennis, called 'Pong', was first released by Atari in 1972, appearing predictable until you got good at it, at which point you could adjust your speed to impact the angle of ricochet in order to defeat your opponent. It was basic, repetitive and one of the hottest games on the market. I was very competitive as a child, equipped with the fiery temperament that some believe comes with red-heads, and with a fellow sports enthusiast for an older brother, we Ponged all summer; I wanted his scalp and grew desperate to perfect the angles off my racket.

Our lives consist of events which cause a reaction, choices we face, and often we find our angle on faith being adjusted as we rebound from their impact. The older we get, the less like a game it feels; things matter more, we believe in less but hold to what remains more passionately. But I invite you to grab the other controller and enter this rebounding world with me because I believe that faith, hope and love each have something to say to one another as we explore how movement in one can adjust our angle of approach to the next. And I feel very grateful for this triangle, not least because it keeps me on my toes like that prehistoric video game. Just as a birth certificate does not prove we are truly living, hospital heart monitors have recently reminded me that flatlined faith is one where no life is evident. My faith feels as though it is, like C.S. Lewis's Aslan, on the move.[3] It has been tried and tested, rebounded and informed, and it feels more alive than ever before. A blue line is being discovered for this spiritual marathon which I cannot run from. Conversely, I may wish to run quickly, as I have become accustomed, but its discovery will not allow me. Tempro is traditionally only of real interest to elite athletes because it represents speed and efficiency, qualities which seem to work against a life of faith, where so much is unseen and patiently awaited.

I want to return again to our three-word triangle through the eyes of Paul. Before concluding with the three remaining priorities of faith, hope and love, the apostle had heard of various problems in the church in the Greek city of Corinth which he had once visited, particularly with the visible outworkings of spiritual gifts. I recognise the quick wins of the visible gifts he lists: speaking in tongues, prophecy, giving to the poor and knowledge. Everybody *notices* these. They are loud gifts. Faith, hope and love, on the other hand, are quiet gifts; their power is unspoken until a life responds, because their volume is only increased when they are personally embodied; actions voicing my outlook upon God and others.

Paul places love at the height of our triangle as the greatest of the three, and he is clear that there is nothing to be gained in the enactment of gifts if love is not present. If you, like me, have spent many years of good intention within the church but became distracted by the approval and recognition to be gained from the use of loud gifts, it is likely that love will have been lost somewhere along the way. You did not mean to, just like you did not mean to drop your car keys in the dark. What we know to be essential is so often misplaced beneath the mounting pile of urgent tasks that appear equally important. So, the blue line must take on this essential characteristic of love; the way in which we must walk and a way in which we must know God. There will be no short cuts, no personal bests (PBs) to be gained, no applause from the crowd, simply the aim to reconnect with our purpose to know God, to know love.

I promised to share weakness, and us runners always have bad races. To date, my worst was the Bupa 10k around London in 2013. The race organisers had erected a PA system just in front of Buckingham Palace as we assembled along The Mall. I had been out late the night before at a concert and not had much sleep, but as the announcer welcomed us all and acknowledged Sir Mo Farah CBE leading the field on a beautiful summer's morning, I was expecting to run well under 45 minutes. In spite of such elite company, seductive weather and scenery, I felt quietly focused and was clear on my pacing strategy, until disaster struck with the starter's siren. The PA system belted out the Queen classic 'Don't Stop Me Now', at which point I disengaged from any game plan and just shot off like the rabbits in neighbouring St James's Park. I don't remember much about the first few kilometres, just being dangerously pumped on life in this convergence of beauty, community and music (always my weaknesses). Silly man.

My composure absent, it was around halfway that I began to suspect I was in trouble. My normal rhythm was not there, I felt laboured and had ceased to enjoy the sights of London around me, with my head dropping lower and lower. I don't give up easily in races, but the run was not enjoyable and became more an act of aggressive will, more mechanical than usual. My target time began to hang over me like a grey cloud instead of a motivation (although I still had not surrendered this as a possibility), but by the final kilometre I got the worst stitch I can remember and reduced speed significantly. The final 200 metres felt most undignified as I hobbled, bent double, shaping a silhouette of a Picasso cubist figure to the finishing line. I could not even hear the crowd but listened to the pain coming from my stitch, thinking I should probably just walk for safety. My brain began nagging: 'How could you be so foolish? You have a wife and family to support! You should no longer be pushing yourself this hard.' I would not walk, I hobbled in. Medal, race T-shirt and banana followed, but they could not disguise the fact that I was disappointed at my lack of self-awareness and failure to achieve my target for a fast 10k. This was not the ending I had had in mind, but neither was a stroke when my wife and family needed me the most.

Since my own season of leadership concluded, I've done a lot in churches over the years, and their leaders have been very gracious and encouraging towards me; leading the music, preaching, Bible studies, mission trips to rough cities and giving hot chocolate to rough sleepers, but not always with the self-awareness to remain humble. Worse still, when you are good at some of these things and people enjoy telling you, even with the best intentions it can go to your head a little. As a guitarist, I've learned some tough lessons along the way, such as the trap of pushing God off the stage, mistaking the guitar groove for his presence amongst his worshippers and the toxic belief that I am being overlooked and under-used in some places I have ended up. Objectively, I think that there remains a place for pointing out shortfalls in the musical worship we create – that the drummer was too obvious, the amp volume at 11 almost broke the glasses of the people sat in the back row, or a bit of rehearsal would have helped – so I still struggle to keep my passion for music that enables others to draw nearer to God a secret from my family's lunch table or my closest friends. The big lesson I must learn and re-learn is humility and that the aim for all leaders of musical worship must surely be to disappear; facilitate then evacuate.

This must be something within my character because I used to be the same with preaching; trying to be the next 'big thing', coming up with the best anecdotes, structuring sermons around stories, shoehorning life into texts that could accommodate my latest joke; then, when the material is used and I had been working too hard, in the pragmatic sense, not having anything left to say when I entered the preaching arena the following week. However many times the mistake was made, I would make it, then make it again. Humility and investment in the work of listening to God, making time for God to speak, are disregarded at huge risk for those who need endorsement, and I confess this weakness in me.

So, the disappointments of seeking approval as a church celebrity and the fame of fast, loud, obvious religion dressed up as service, now leave me confronted with the slow place of this triangle which I have come to reluctantly acknowledge as a runner *without* a church to lead. I have to be still in order to know;[4] to stop my activity if things are to occur to me. Like preparing for a marathon, there must be time invested when no one is looking – difficult for someone like me who thrives in teams or seeks approval. But at the point of this third stroke, there I was once again, lying on my back in King's College Hospital, questioning God, surprised at the absence of karma within Christianity: 'What more can I do, God? I try to be kind to others. I trained as a minister in The Salvation Army,

I led two churches and loved the people with every minute of my life. Don't forget that morning, God, where I stopped on a run and bought three stoned homeless men some cookies in a petrol station with the only change I had in my pocket! You remember, when the guy asked if they were flammable!' Random thoughts bombard the mind when your salvation project is cut short and God's love appears as a cruel joke; our faith crudely jolted like a new driver accelerating only to shift down from fourth into third by mistake, as we lurch forwards yet are held back.

But in this place of ridiculous bargaining and mental bombardment, I did not feel trapped. Taking a deep breath, I knew that there was a quality to the soft perimeter of this triangle. There is no fence keeping me in, I am allowed to wander wherever I please, rebounding between faith, hope and love – three words which won't leave me – before finally, of my own free will, discovering that an available water trough lies at its centre. I always seem to end up at the well, exhausted and parched, sometimes with a stitch, like a racehorse brought into paddock whose deep breath forms clouds of smoke on a crisp winter morning, having given everything on the track. It was at the third stroke that I chose to drink more slowly and remembered that the greatest gift God gives is love.

2

A Running God

Peter, however, got up and ran to the tomb.[1]

This chapter is about shame, grace and the truth about God. Haruki Murakami is a Japanese runner and writer who describes beautifully the difference between living in a fog or living with clear goals that come from distance running. It is the clearing of this fog that I have personally felt for years as a runner, like a switching on of my entire body or a mental and physical recharging of my battery. Murakami also knows the sarcastic comments that come to people who run every day from those who believe that they are in an exhausting pursuit of living longer. He believes this to be untrue; he thinks most people's motivation for running is to live a deeper, richer life.[2] For me, running is transformative yet one of the simplest things I can do, so I just run, and when I do, something takes over and I feel peaceful about my life. I run because *I can*, because my legs will do it, because I have the strength in my body to perform this activity that I know many, through age, injury or ill-health do not. But I am not addicted to running, it is not a god. In fact, there are even days when I have to be disciplined to do it, but it represents a convergence of body and mind that brings me into alignment with the world, my family, my work; a place I choose to call meeting with God.

In the past I once ran away from meeting with God. Attending an Alpha course Holy Spirit away day in my early twenties on a college campus, one of my friends was praying in a typically sedate room of people. Moments later I could hear crying (not unusual for church groups when space is created for spiritual recalibration) before this soon turned into uncontrollable laughter. I felt uncomfortable, not because we were British and culturally restrained, but because the noise was liberated beyond convention and an expression of freedom I had never encountered. I ran from the room, half-embarrassed for him and half-terrified, making it to a friend's flat nearby. Gordon Cotterill has always been there for me, wise beyond his years and a perennial pace-setter for my own discipleship. After frantically knocking at his door, he opened it with the words, 'Oz, are you OK? You look like you've seen a ghost.' It was the first time I had seen the Holy Ghost manifest in this way; I wanted reasons, answers, and stunned to the edge of tears, I had chosen to run.

These days, I tend to run towards God. This is precisely because he represents mystery and something larger than myself to which I am drawn. As I have aged, I have grown more interested in what I term 'big things', either material or emotional, anything appearing larger than my control or realm of knowledge and experience; jumbo jets and space rockets, journeys of endurance, courageous demonstrations of those who push themselves against the odds, exploring new frontiers and going where few get to travel physically or mentally within unpredictably fine margins. In my small way, the joy of running, especially the treat of five months of marathon training, puts me into a focused season of life where I get to touch something relatively unknown to most, with a small element of risk involved but nonetheless beyond ordinary.

When I run far, the defences tumble and my outlook is broadened. I might see shafts of light breaking through a forest of trees, or a sunset airbrushing clouds with a fiery palette of pink and orange, and then remember that God is surprising, awe-inspiring, even humorous to me. Why would anyone be so generous as to create such missable beauty for an audience of one? Is this not wasteful, like an extraordinary fish swimming in darkness at the bottom of the deepest ocean, that only modern technology has unearthed for our living room satisfaction? But it swims all the same, it exists while I do, and probably then some. With so many deep blue questions about 'big things', my outlook on a broadening world is constantly changing.

In this chapter, the characters who run in the resurrection of Christ narrative experienced something which broadened their outlook. It was absorbing yet shocking, fearing the repercussions yet being drawn towards the potential of God's activity; magnets where union with God is, while difficult, yet a mere flip of poles away. How often we do not realise what we have until it's too late, or God's presence is just the other side of our fears, thinly veiled, tantalisingly discoverable. There is a song on my running playlist by an English rock band called Elbow which encapsulates this sentiment. It nostalgically describes the joy of teenage possibilities of such golden days with lyrics urging every boy to construct a rocket.[3] In very basic terms, as a husband and father with grown-up responsibilities, often tempted to regard myself with inflated self-importance, something such as outer space trumps my little domesticated realm and represents life beyond my control; very healthy for remembering one's place in this universe. To build a rocket is a perfect expression of joy when the world lies at your feet. The day British astronaut Tim Peake rocket-launched from earth, bound for the International Space Station, I was attempting to launch off the sofa post-surgery. I felt alive again, hoping that more golden days of running were to come and I could delve deeper into relationship with a big God.

The impact of running upon my outlook on life has been with me since childhood, although the first time it happened was something of an accident. I never enjoyed gymnastics at primary school, always finding the back of the queue for gymnastics or physical education activities requiring any kind of upside-down manoeuvre. To my mind, the world ought to stay upright as far as possible. But then came a sports day in the local park where the headteacher, a very tall man wearing glasses whose deep voice and choice of words brought formality to every occasion, decided that the older boys would run a race over 220 yards. I remember thinking, 'I'm not sure how far a yard is!' but I was fascinated by the rope layout of the grassy course because it had a turn in it where we would hairpin back on ourselves. The only event where I had seen a similar course where I could imagine silence but great anticipation was the Grand National. Looking at the undulating grass ahead of me, I worked out that this distance required something to be left in the tank for after that bend, very different to the frenzy of the 100 metres sprint. Thirty-three years ago, and it's like this race was yesterday (I have butterflies in my stomach as I write)! The headteacher began the race, parents cheered and I started fast, but more significantly, I *stayed* fast. I must have judged the speed perfectly because energy built upon energy and, after that hairpin, I pulled away from my primary school rivals, feeling the tape and a first taste of success in this most surprising sphere of running. I felt a sense of completion and contentment; all was well with my soul.[4]

My inclinations towards running continued into secondary education, where I made a friend who was so smart that he had morphed into a walking dictionary by the time we sat GCSEs. I remember a farewell note that he wrote to me on leaving the sixth form which poetically said he hoped that every football felt the net, in stark contrast to the brash 'Good luck, mate!' which most teenagers creatively churn out in clumsy marker pen. He possessed an amazing knowledge of the Old Testament, which shone through in art history classes long before faith stories truly mattered to me. But the only upper hand I had was that he couldn't run; he had no interest in it, lacked any coordinated arm and leg rhythm and a style that resembled man's first strides upon the moon. I was encouraged by his awkward bounce because at least here was one thing I could do better than him. To him, running was pointless and so unnecessary.

I had been building memories which led to an enjoyment of the feeling of running and an awareness that my own speed was enough to get me towards the 'above-average' standard amongst my classmates. I liked to test it from time to time, such as my re-enactment on holiday as a seven-year-old of the 1981 film *Chariots of Fire* with a head swirling with Vangelis's powerful electric drone, which caused me to sprint along a coastal path and crash straight through my brother's brand-new kite. In a catastrophic compound of enthusiasm and a turn in the weather, the kite's trajectory dipped perfectly into my path on its maiden flight; one moment we were soaring, the next the breeze and my heart had dropped.

As I consider how my running informs my belief in God – through the feelings it creates in me or the reasons behind this – I join good company in the New Testament in which the apostle Paul is quoted as choosing to use 'running my race'[5] as a metaphor for his quest to preach the good news of Christ to the Gentiles and encouraging others in this task, with words such as 'You were running a good race'.[6] Of course, we also hear of politicians on campaign trails 'running' for office today. So, running can be seen as life lived deliberately.

As I have hinted at already, the Bible also contains useful examples of people, like me, who ran as their personal reaction to the presence of Jesus. There is running in fear upon Jesus' arrest as his followers fled faster than you could say 'Gethsemane', to which I could certainly relate in my college away day. But our main running event for this chapter is when Mary Magdalene ran in resurrection confusion. She was bewildered after visiting the tomb in which Jesus' body was buried, only to find it empty. Her thoughts travelling at light speed, what does her body immediately do but run? Perhaps in panic, she needs to share the dramatic sight she has seen, 'So she came running to Simon Peter and the other disciple, the one Jesus loved, and said, "They have taken the Lord out of the tomb, and we don't know where they have put him!"'[7] Mary ran because she could not contain her experience, either suspecting foul play from the Roman authorities or anxious that the script had reached its hairpin moment.

After witness of the empty tomb is first reported by 'Mary Magdalene, Joanna' and 'Mary the mother of James',[8] we then see a running race between two of Jesus' followers, 'Both were running, but the other disciple outran Peter and reached the tomb first.'[9] This is running in hope. Two disciples who can get no satisfaction from what they have just heard about rolling stones must see for themselves. It is our desperation to see beyond them or our refusal to surrender to the apparent failures in our lives that can cause us to run, sometimes towards evidence, at other times, away from it.

For Peter, a disciple who had pledged loyalty but fled after denying Christ three times, passions ran high and running was probably in his character. Having run away from Christ but run towards the empty tomb, Peter was finally still enough to be treated to a beach barbecue by the resurrected Christ.[10] After all this running, I can imagine Christ's question over cooked fish: 'So, now you have caught your breath, what are you going to do with the rest of your life?' It is the kind of question which may have greeted the prodigal son, the morning after returning to his father, except in the prodigal's case, the father was the one out of breath. Jesus paints a picture of the countercultural forgiveness of God through this parable, represented by the waiting father who is also a runner. 'But while he was still a long way off, his father saw him and was filled with compassion for him; he ran to his son, threw his arms round him and kissed him.'[11] The father runs; God runs. This time it is not the seeker or wanderer doing the chasing, rather the opposite – the son walks in shame, a defenceless Jew after wasting his inheritance among Gentiles. The father leaves the doorstep of his own estate in his impulse to run and publicly embrace his returning son.

The significance of this only becomes clear when we understand the cultural boundaries of a running father. In order to gain speed, his tunic would have to be pulled up to reveal bare legs – humiliating for a first-century Middle Eastern man. After this, the father desires to reach his son before the community get to him, for if a Jewish son has wasted an inheritance among Gentiles then a shaming ceremony would be performed. The 'qetsatsah' enactment saw the shattering of a large earthenware jug (filled with corn and burnt nuts) at the feet of the guilty, yelling words to reinforce that he was cut off from his own people,[12] just in case he needed reminding that his life story, a jagged yet recent past, lay smashed in many pieces. Jesus uses this parable to teach his listeners about the reconciliation available in God; a shocking conclusion to religious ears and not the God they were banking upon. Understood to be the divine initiative of 'grace', the God revealed by Christ, as we will see in later chapters, is a gracious God. This is the opposite of hoping in a religious karma which had initially bombarded my private hospital thoughts around the flint and steel of pain rubbing against the grain of God's goodness. I am thrilled that Jesus' parable mentions running because it represents how this God of grace needed to beat the crowds of karma. Followers of Jesus run – sometimes in fear, confusion, desperation or hope, but better than that, Christ points them towards a gracious Father who also happens to be a running God.

This link between the body and spirit fascinates me, as I hope it will you. Although I cannot pretend to keep pace or always understand the deeply reflective yet ever-popular writings of Franciscan Father Richard Rohr, he too considers matter and spirit as inseparable in Christ, 'giving us the courage and insight to acknowledge and honor the same in ourselves.'[13] At last, permission to breathe, to sweat, to be an activist like Peter, running to see more of God, like bewildered disciples to a tomb or shepherds to a manger. This book rests upon a personal realisation that if I am to write about God, then I must write about his and my running.

3

Roads to Damascus and Roads to Emmaus

As he neared Damascus on his journey, suddenly a light from heaven flashed around him.[1]

You don't have to spend too long in bookshops, doctors' surgeries or looking at supermarket packaging to absorb the message that there is a cry for wellbeing ringing throughout society. Actually, living in our pressurised Western environment, standing alone wishing that our bridges truly connected us to one another, it's more of a Munch scream than a cry.[2] I believe that one of the reasons mental health has climbed the agenda is that we have less time to think, less space to digest what is happening to the world around us and consequently less ability to respond meaningfully to it. Our relationships suffer through a lack of pause and the underdevelopment of our skills of listening, reflecting and adjusting our behaviour. This stunts the formation of our emotional intelligence, a necessary skill if we are going to achieve our potential in life as much as sheer IQ,[3] but equally our receptivity to anything spiritual. I confess that I am distracted too. What hope do I have of listening through prayer if I cannot even listen to my wife without jumping to the bleep of mobile device notifications? Consequently, there seem to be two colliding spheres of attentiveness; at first blush, the Bible appears to be loaded with moments where people encountered

God in various tangible ways with extreme regularity; visions
and voices for the lucky lead characters. But my life has never
been such a lively play as this, though I have often craved it,
which has made me examine the then and now. Even when we
try to be attentive, why do we not experience God so often?

I find part of the answer in talking about one of life's
necessities – journeys, a word that has become overused as a
metaphor which once simply implied geographical movement
from A to B. The world to which Christ came was a world on
foot for the majority, a world in which travelling provided the
time to think. This chapter began with a reference to Saul, the
most passionate of critics of the first disciples, who encountered
Jesus through dazzling light and challenging words as he travelled towards Damascus. Mary and Joseph had many hours to
ponder the imminence of Christ's arrival, to wrestle and share
their hearts, as they journeyed to Bethlehem that first Christmas; to give each other not just the freedom to speak but the
freedom to be silent in one another's company. Now, how often
does that happen in our moments of uncertainty today, when
the temptation to grab the television remote seems stronger?
I maintain that running addresses this lack of attentiveness,
where I can be surrounded by thousands in my silence, yet
this silence is perfectly acceptable. While I tune in to my body
and listen to its twinges, it does not allow me to flit towards
anything else; consequently, this has become a very precious
time of solitude as I jog the roads from A to B. Steps take time;
when you are learning to walk again you appreciate this, and
the average marathon uses between 25–30,000 strides over 26
miles 385 yards,[4] which is a lot of time to think. I don't need
the latest bumper book of 'Mindfulness colouring-in pictures',

because I have learned that over time God meets me in some form, like Saul, journeying along roads.

In our previous family homes, a rumbling fanfare has announced my mother-in-law when she comes to stay; the sound of suitcase wheels on concrete paths, edging closer to the front door. To my amusement, when my daughter was very young she mimicked this, whether arriving at a holiday house in Wales after a long summer trip along the M4, or if we were literally driving ten minutes around the corner and all the wheeled case held was a pad of A4 – mindfulness colouring, probably. If the suitcase could come with us, it did, symbolising the intent to pack, travel and arrive. I once asked Grandma if she preferred the journey compared to the destination (I had an idea what her answer might be) and yes, the journey by train with coffee, sandwich and newspaper was indeed the best bit. Travelling means momentum because outlook shifts, the scenery changes and the difference becomes intriguing to the mind.

But what if we never *arrived* anywhere? As I consider the forty years of wandering for the Israelites who followed Moses, it is almost impossible to comprehend that a whole lifetime could be spent trusting a promise but never seeing the land that was talked about along the way. It is amazing how far we can walk when we insist on moving in circles, taking much time but achieving little progress. Moses never entered the Promised Land; that delight was Joshua's. It takes courage to accept that the journey for some may be the actual point. Back then, believing meant following, holding on through the days of doubt, trusting that something meaningful would one day come. Resigning one's self to a life on the move. Surely, life is still thus for most of us.

Perhaps much anxiety exists today because we expect too much from life; we want arrival, success, a slice of the action. Our menu and prayers not only include a standard lifespan (ever-increasing due to medical research) but finding the time to fit in the best social life, family life, career life and overcoming adversity by climbing Everest-life. Encounter with God becomes relegated either to the small print or when my plan comes off and I regard it as his silent endorsement. Yet again, I'm also guilty of this tempting crammed-full life. We are all equally under pressure to present our story online, a parallel digital existence which may one day turn into that motivational book that breaks records in Waterstone's, more so than mindfulness has done, leaving an ordinary existence for dust. Presenting our lives in this way, becoming our own advertising agencies, fielding the responses, is not only time-consuming but can lead to madness as we forfeit the reality under our noses. Suddenly, spiritually blindfolded, we have wandered down a road that does not withstand the slow journey, preferring to present our story not as a workshop, but within a gallery reserved for masters. We digitally post the final oil paintings, but a wandering Israel lived through the sketch, the hard effort, the early ideas and inclinations of following God, whoever and wherever he happened to be.

We runners spend hours on roads. Given our dilemma, there are two very different examples of people encountering Christ along roads which I would like to explore – Damascus and Emmaus. Damascus is dramatic, with bright lights, voices, unmistakable divinity, blindness and the spectacularly transformed character of our 'faith, hope and love' author at the start of this book – Paul, formerly referred to as Saul until sometime after his dramatic conversion. Emmaus, on the other hand, is routine. We will know it as a necessary journey of crestfallen disciples with a stranger who appears to be the only person not to have read a newspaper. They see Christ from a base of low expectation and gradual realisation.[5] What links these two opposing roads is reformed character; two experiences with the same outcome of meeting Christ. Damascus roads are probably more in tune with competitive runners, those who become obsessed with PBs, pacing mile splits to the second on our watches to achieve targets we've often dreamt of and with boring our families with all our race stories. Emmaus roads are more gradual, unspectacular, the journey of the long-distance runner.

Growing up in The Salvation Army and being part of its brass band culture inevitably meant time spent walking along roads, whether marching down London's Oxford Street to the thump of a bass drum or standing at the Whitehall Cenotaph on Remembrance Sunday. I was a cornet player and took part in outdoor evangelism three times each Sunday, giving me the chance to navigate potholes and walk many miles of tarmac through the capital. I would guess that Salvation Army bandsmen have the best knowledge of London's streets second only to Hackney carriage drivers. There were both fond memories and humorous ones of my church – Regent Hall Corps, as it is known today; the moment our bass drum player (who was on the short side yet could hit the huge instrument strapped to his chest as hard as anyone) failed to see a bollard and managed to mount it instead, to the multiple flashes of tourist cameras. Perhaps this has never happened in Japan? There was the triumphalism of marching behind a huge wooden cross on Easter Sunday, leaving Londoners in no doubt that these fifty or so rank-and-file Salvationists meant business when it meant proclaiming Christ was risen. Then there was the thrill of Christmas, taking to the streets in our white-gloved uniforms which would reflect the Regent Street Christmas lights above with the choreographed buoyancy of Disney's 'Sorcerer's Apprentice'. It was collegiate and I felt safe; toasted teacakes for supper tasted sweeter after a day serving God so boldly.

But I wasn't interested in finding any Tempro along those roads, of keeping in step with God, not back then; happy to ride the wave of triumphant religious expression supported by a sizeable youth group and musical role models. A turning point came on the day I met my wife who, as part of that group, was also a music student at Royal Holloway College in Egham, Surrey. Similarly from Salvationist stock, she was experiencing the benefit of a university Christian Union which challenged inherited belief and encouraged individual faith. I could not have stumbled across a more different person to myself: she was humble, considered, an excellent listener and very careful with words. Her restraint and challenging of my careless use of language and humour (often blasphemous) spoke to me as clearly as light dawning. It still does. I *knew* about Christianity but suddenly I saw it, much like Saul, and it wouldn't let me go. God had got to work; I was travelling a new road.

Our early years together involved a lot of commuting, jumping on and off trains in and out of London, snatching a hot chocolate at Waterloo station before separating to commence another working week. At the time I was a student at Central Saint Martins College of Art and Design, a vacuum of postmodern dialogue which challenged all views of the world through art while replacing them with nothing. This moral abyss was the first anvil upon which my faith was formed. Nobody believed in absolutes and nothing was off-limits; sexuality and identity were the recurring themes and I was just grateful for Helen, prayer and a degree of stability, because the day we met ended quite extraordinarily. That evening, alone in my bedroom, I read Nicky Gumbel's *Why Jesus?*[6] (a throwaway booklet destined for the bin following a self-imposed spring clean). I was transfixed by its news. I suddenly *saw* that, in Christ, God had come, and I was known and loved. An infinite peace overwhelmed me; I knew all would be well. A sudden awakening so unexpected, absolute truth breaking into my assumed post-modernity. This was not in my script whatsoever; so vast a rerouting, yet so simple. It also felt so unlike me; the irony of a Damascus-road moment breaking into the life of a sceptical teenager, but I was unwittingly ready because in truth I had been questioning the reality of God for some months beneath the protection of a Salvationist's uniform and was hungry to find him.

Perhaps this is why Saul's life was also so dramatically changed along his Damascus road, his head loaded with arguments against Christ and zealous in his persecution of his followers. He had at least been thinking it through without noticing God's creeping towards his misplaced passions. I remember waking up the following morning and reading the words of Thomas, to whom Jesus said 'blessed are those who have not seen and yet have believed'.[7] This was written for me and I could not deny it. All the way to art college on the train I could only think about Jesus, my new hope who had reached down to such a sceptic as me. My middle name is Thomas so I connected on this level too. I thought of David Bowie's 'Space Oddity' and the voice bridging earth and outer space; so it was as if God had built a bridge between heaven and earth and first contact had been achieved with me, a minor 'Thomas', on that night – 21 March 1994. The date is engraved inside our wedding rings.

Out of the blocks with such pace, it then seemed that Damascus-road moments were to become the norm, although I now realise that this is not the case with Christianity. There is nothing more annoying than a Christian trying to convince everybody else that Christ is true, particularly during zealous early years, unless God intervenes and changes a person from the inside. This transaction cannot be forced; one at best facilitates, but where no hunger exists, who needs bread? However, another Damascus did come my way when I began to ask God for his opinion on where my life should be spent, or *his* life actually. I soon became surrounded by murmurings that I should put myself forward for leadership training in The Salvation Army, 'Officership', which involved two years of residential training at the William Booth College on London's Denmark Hill, Camberwell. The idea seemed to make sense, marrying my new-found passion with a personal love of public speaking, and very conveniently was the future road my wife had discerned she should take. But it required something of Salvationist terminology – '*the* call', an obscure, mystical term that I genuinely began to fear missing or not being able to discern amongst the clamour of encouragers who saw passion and immediately equated it with leadership. *The* call, opposed to *a* call which one can find dotted throughout Scripture, was only reserved for some. It seemed to happen quite rarely (judging by the number of people who actually responded to it) and it held a bit of a stigma as marking you out as 'religious', somewhat like clergy caricatured by laity. In many people's eyes, the call was uncool.

But I knew, and still do, that my life was God's gift, so I prayed and waited, listened and watched. I heard and saw nothing.

I checked my intentions (no, my wife's 'call' was personal to her) and gradually became quite agonised over the whole process. With a tendency for overthinking things, my thoughts of it began to work against doing it as my own voice drowned out the poise needed to hear God's. Until one evening, that is. With my wife's road chosen and the unresolved tension of our future together, I had decided to agree for a cabin counsellor position[8] in the United States of America for the following summer, which would mean a couple of months living abroad with time and space to think alone. I hastened to get to the home of my interviewer one evening after college and in my fatigue had managed to board the wrong half of a train which divided at the stop before my destination. As we pulled into the station and I phoned her to explain that I would be late, she surprisingly told me in no uncertain terms that if I couldn't get to Dulwich to meet an adult, then how could I be trusted to get to America to supervise children? I can only assume that she had been having a difficult day too.

Interview abandoned and hopes dented, I returned to the platform to wait for my train home and looked up at the night sky feeling like the confidence to work with children had been sucked out of me by a solitary sentence. I had ended up at Denmark Hill station and was sitting alone in my own thoughts, confused about the plans of God (as normal), directly opposite the illuminated crucifix which decorates the brick façade of the William Booth College tower, dominating that part of London's skyline and glorifying the evening sky. I felt an odd resonance, a feeling of being targeted, right place and right time, some would say. But it was enough to remind me that God knew where and who I was and how much I wanted his purposes for me and my decision-making. Bizarrely for a sceptic, and one who's train had taken the wrong road, sitting on a railway bench at Denmark Hill station was another moment of *knowing*. That night, with right-minded reasoning, a weighing up of circumstance, the laying down of passions in admittance of new ones, I concluded that God had called me to become an Officer; *the* call had come.

In the following weeks, and with the last traces of self-belief I could muster, I pursued my original aim of working abroad. Via a different route, and some months later, there I was working with children in California on a camp run by The Salvation Army, discovering more about the world and asking God for his views as I went. It's been a tricky life, the life of prayer; you cannot trust feelings. For me it became a silent subtext for my life on the go helping those kids from gangs, listening to their tears and stopping them from killing each other with rocks inside pillowcases swung around their heads at midnight. I just had to consciously give the day to God then get on with it. Reality cares little for neat quiet times; I just had to find quietness wherever I could, with as little sleep second only to having a newborn child in one's house.

It was while in America that I too gave God the space to direct my path with marriage. Lifelong commitment had been something I was afraid of; could not trust myself with. I mean, what do you do on the bad days when you just don't *feel* like loving? I had no experience of this, apart from the love of Christ which had completely upturned my previous notions, showing that the dots join to form a picture not of feelings but of choice – the choice to love. Damascus-road guidance continued (God must have known I needed baby food); firstly, when a boys-only scouting camp meant we had to swap campsites with the neighbouring girls-only Guides camp, and I found myself in a cabin previously occupied by a counsellor named Helen. Her most recent group of teenagers had made her colourful, glittery posters which adorned the walls, so everywhere I looked all I could see, apart from the occasional mouse, was the emblazoned name 'Helen'.

A few days later I booked a haircut on a day off in a small barber's, close to Malibu beach. I have never really liked hairdressers; I almost prefer the dentist, because at least with the latter you have an excuse not to talk, but as I sat, imprisoned in the chair of small talk, the business card of the hairdresser was staring back at me, 'Helen'. I made a second mental note, smiling.

Now before I reel off incident number three, Helen was beautiful, inside and out, and I knew I didn't want to let her life be the joy of another man. She had got under my skin and I was entering new territory. In truth, I was delaying the inevitable.

Much like buses arriving at once, event number three occurred when I was travelling back from America and needed an overnight stay in New York. Booking into a Salvation Army hostel over the phone (not normal practice but I was a British backpacker in need of cheap accommodation), I asked for the name of the receptionist pulling the strings, who replied . . . I won't even bother. It was a strange season of watching for the activity of God, a period of life where more was dictated to me by him. Damascus road after Damascus road, you could say. It would be impossible to live permanently in this manner – what if you missed a sign or made a wrong turn? – and too much like *The Truman Show*,[9] a fabricated Christianity that does not allow for creativity or renewal through change. I remember when my son first realised the absence of the commentator's voice when he attended a real football match, standing there on the terraces asking, 'Dad, where's the big voice?' Its absence initially hard to swallow, reality takes much more work, and so does the life of a disciple.

Before we move from Damascus to Emmaus, another significant change which occurred during that American summer was my decision to leave the brass banding behind for now, upon my return to my London corps. The same was true for another of my closest friends, Matt Spencer, a trombonist who remains a soulmate since our shared summer of working together and willingness to write music with me to this day. I had not departed with this in mind, and as an eclectic music lover, the sound of brass at the highest levels of excellence remains thrilling today, but our eyes had been opened and our hands were freshly cut upon the broken fragments of the lives of others; I could no longer take my anonymous place within the jubilant banding brigade. There was a disquiet birthed within me about the impotence of my Sabbath duty; it was too easy and kept reality at arm's length. Everything I said I was about had no space within my routine. Change had to come, so I took my place amongst the congregation of my church and began to work at crossing the participant-audience divide. This in itself became part of the preparation for Officership enabling me to befriend the elderly, the homeless or recovering alcoholics, people with issues well beyond my comfort zone. It was a time of rapid growth, theology being pushed and pulled as my new-found squeaky-clean God of love was dragged through the dirt. How quickly I was learning that Damascus roads, while being jubilant and wonderful and life-changing and ecstatic, are not the end of the journey. Instead, as I was finding, they are often only the start.

I am sat writing this chapter on a very cold January morning and I have been looking out of the window at two runners who have obviously met on the hour. Runners are people of precision, rarely late, it seems, and to whom split seconds really matter. They are wrapped up in hats, gloves and moving on the spot while my still body wakes up at a desk with the usual prescription of tablets and a hot cup of tea. This drink needs to be respected; tea can be friend and foe. Once discharged from hospital after my first craniotomy, I was more troubled by heartburn than headaches for the first couple of days, a pain so discomforting that I could not sleep and felt like the left side of my chest could explode at any moment. Of course, there was nothing medically wrong but thanks to the reassurance of Google I understood this to be probably due to a caffeine over-dose from hospital cups of tea. Where there's not much to do except wait for a doctor with an update on your body's progress or the latest test result, the serving of tea is quite an event.

Turning back to my cold runners in the park, they appear to be waiting for someone as they regularly look in one direction down the street, chatting as they stretch. Eventually time is up, they decide to set off – two committed men, perhaps intended to be three; only they know, as they run off into the distance between a tunnel of almost overhanging bare trees.

Two often talk, and a question was once shared between two of Christ's disciples after they had walked the road from Jeru-salem to a village called Emmaus, approximately 7 miles away, 'Were not our hearts burning within us while he talked with us on the road . . . ?'[10] It is three days since Christ's crucifixion, and en route, one of the travellers, Cleopas, is drawn into a conversation with a stranger who is unaware of recent events, so Cleopas shares his dashed hopes about Jesus and accelerating puzzlement at reports of an empty tomb. They stop and invite the stranger in, for it is 'nearly evening',[11] yet they have no idea that this invitation is about to cause the best kind of heartburn they've ever had.

The Supper at Emmaus is one of my favourite paintings, executed in oil and tempera by the Italian artist Michelangelo Merisi da Caravaggio and commissioned by the Roman nobleman Ciriaco Mattei in 1601. Housed in London's National Gallery, it depicts the moment Christ (the walking stranger) blesses the bread and reveals his true identity to the two disciples. I like the work for two reasons; artistically, Caravaggio uses light and shadow to convey the intense drama of what is taking place; Christ is light in their darkness, echoed by the shadows cast by objects on the table depicting him as the source of light. I like the body language too: the disciple on the right opens his arms wide in shock, almost mimicking the recent crucifixion pose in which he possibly last saw Christ (also giving Caravaggio the chance to show his skill at foreshortening to the world as the hand nearest the viewer reaches out towards us). The other disciple grips his own chair, possibly poised to stand or to steady himself from fainting at the revelation before his eyes.

But I like this painting personally because of its layout, composed to invite us in and transform our role from viewer to participant in its almost 2-metre width of frame and open-sided table. Stepping into the picture frame, it depicts the second type of way in which I have found Christ to meet me – along Emmaus roads. Here God comes alongside in moments of honest sharing or recuperation with others, times when we feel the least deserving, the most vulnerable, times when our expectations are at their lowest. I'm calling these moments the 'Emmaus shift' because the roles are reversed. We, thinking we are inviting Christ in as guest, unexpectedly become guest and he becomes our host. I don't know how many times I need to learn this lesson until I truly live it out, but if you put others first, invite them in, share your life with them, it seems to me that God mysteriously becomes more tangible and gives us a deeper reassurance of his presence. Perhaps hospitality uncovers some of the blue Tempro line we crave?

I first experienced an Emmaus shift in 2010. It was new year, and I was on my way down from Yorkshire to Kent for meetings before becoming a classroom teacher in a primary school. Leaving behind a ministry in church leadership, it was with a heavy heart that I squinted through the windscreen wipers on my car, which seemed to be clearing both snow and tears. Halfway through my winter's journey and after two hours in my own head, reasoning back and forth like a competitive rower, I needed a coffee and pulled into a motorway service station. I find such places impersonal and draughty, almost designed to either propel you back to your car as quickly as possible, or make you buy more coffee. The gambling machines, the unswept floor, the tired-looking doughnuts behind the smeared glass counter on the forecourt – can anything good truly grow from this mundane, lifeless scene? In truth, I was only there because I was exploring vocation and unsure of my next step, somewhat disorientated by the past and where following 'the call' had led me. Much like Cleopas and the other disciple, God hadn't been as active as I would have hoped, and circumstances made him seem like a boxer finally on the canvas, but this time not getting up. Compounded against the background of this soulless place, I was making my walk to Emmaus.

Once inside the service station, hidden in my anonymity, my eyes happened to meet the gaze of an old friend who was also purchasing a cup of coffee from the same counter. Despite being on in years and probably retired, his eyes retained the sincerity I had witnessed more than twenty years previously when he had trained a brass band I played in at one of The Salvation Army's summer schools for young musicians. He was an expressive, motivational and often unorthodox bandleader, quite happy to drop the baton and let the tears flow from his eyes if the music ambushed him, such was his depth of faith behind the musical score. On one occasion, he just wept in a concert, having done the hard work by then and knowing that we, the band, could be left to autopilot. I think he wept at the fulfilled musical potential of teenagers; that's how much the generational passing on of the baton meant to him.

I always enjoy unorthodox personalities with a sense of humour, and he still had this. He had some denominational fame as a trombonist whereas I was a mere back-bencher on the brass scene, but once we had both recovered from the odd coincidence of this chance encounter, we were very much on a level footing; separated by generations, missiology, strategic outlook on the future of The Salvation Army, personal experience – who knows, who cares? – none of it mattered. Words flowed with the coffee as we shared our journeys and reasons for travel. In true fashion, his life that evening involved leading a trombone masterclass, whereas I confessed that mine was sliding into very unexpected territory. Making the most of this opportunity, I began to open up to this representative of the tradition and history of The Salvation Army from my rather limp lifetime's supreme service as an Officer of seven years; my fears of letting people down, of letting *God* down as I contemplated leaving church leadership to step through the cascade of opening doors that were leading me back towards the classroom. As Don listened, his eyes filled with tears (of course).

The sharp edge to this process is that when one becomes an Officer, a covenantal pledge is made for a lifetime of service, to 'love and serve him supremely all my days'[12] and I was breaking this pledge. I had not consciously decided to serve anything else, nor someone else, I was not on any clear route out of leadership, there was no angry rebellion. I was just attempting to follow God down this unexpected road with all the faith I could gather. I had dared to ask the question of 'What next along this road?' of following him, and each time it felt like life staying put was easy, too easy.

It is an odd place to be when you never saw it coming, bringing loneliness and feelings of disloyalty and hurt to those who have invested so much in you, but I am comforted by the similar experiences of others who, as true friends, have opened up to weakness on this issue. My friend Thomas Anderson, a Salvation Army Officer in Oslo, Norway (home of Munch's *Scream* painting to which I earlier referred), put his own need to move from a church leadership role in similar terms: 'It was safe for me to stay, I was afraid I would become stuck . . . not challenge myself. It was like a personal development moment for me. I'm afraid of the routine.' One of Thomas' Officer-ship appointments saw him drained after a seven-year project merging two corps into one in the centre of Halden, a town of 30,000 people. Speaking with him in February 2019 he expressed this process with the words: 'I felt that my work was done. I had maintained a vision, upheld it, been the lone moti-vator. I would rebound between hopelessness and hope.' How has he survived? For Thomas, calling is actually very simple. 'Jesus simply says "Come, follow me,"'[13] showing that he has

escaped the shackles of denominational loyalty or any other
emotional pressures to remain. In that confidence, he continues as an Officer today. Our conversation reminded me how
similar we are, both musicians (Thomas has a velvet voice – I
don't) with a weakness for the spotlight and craving for success,
but we seem to have arrived at the same point in life where we
accept that 'some of us are just normal people . . . most of us
do our work silently in the shadows'. You could argue, different
routes leading to the same Emmaus road.

Back to the service station and sitting together, I felt one of
my most acute spiritual struggles; vulnerable with nothing to
lean on, reputation, skills and talents barely glowing under the
rubble of circumstance and just open-mindedness to God as
guide. I was in two minds, attracted to the adventure yet wanting to pull back in equal measure. My bandmaster just listened;
he could see my pain. He had the expression of someone who
had come across his own endings. He stared without judgement, just looked me straight in the eye and, once I'd finished,
clearly told me that my covenant remained true.

I cannot express how much I needed to hear Don's simple endorsement that evening, but the pose of Caravaggio's
chair-grabber paints the drama well enough. I had entered the
Emmaus picture plane. His voice was gentle, yet had authority.
When such a message is delivered from the most unexpected
source, hints of fabrication, of forcing square pegs into round
holes, of asking people about God's will until you get the answer you want to hear, are frankly blown out of the water. From
that moment on, I once again knew all would be well. I think
Don could hear my continuing desire to serve God supremely
and love his people, despite the fork in the road that had led
me down the A1. I had wandered in feeling little connection

with the God I once pledged to serve, like a disgraced prodigal imagining repercussions for deliberate choices, for seizing back control from a loving Father. But an Emmaus shift had taken place where Don had in fact hosted me and through this exchange, I chose to believe that I had heard from God. I walked out to the car, praising God's ever-presence.

Like the two Emmaus disciples who returned immediately to Jerusalem (which incidentally meant another seven-mile walk into the night), I celebrated by phoning my wife to share my joy at this intersection intercession. Around that time of new year, with Christmas decorations not quite lofted away, angels normally appear as sprinkled cinnamon sieved onto the froth of coffee. But back on the road, I knew that one had just come to sit with me.

The boost that one receives from such moments of divine intervention is breathtaking. It is enough to get you saying and doing things you wouldn't do normally, crediting and worshipping God with renewed freedom. Such injections of a burning heart into ordinary life arrive as gifts. Faith to an atheist must seem like such a rash, foolish move, but for me, Christianity is not an abandonment of intelligence or a choice just to believe the next hit along the catwalk of spiritual fashion. Faith is a reasoned response to gifts; the activity of God, both in history and the present, often only seeing the next few steps of illumination (like a runner in the night with a headtorch) and deciding to continue in the manner which I have set out. Like a marathoner after a water station, my Emmaus shift left me positive and determined to continue. It must sound ridiculous to others, but such moments are akin to déjà vu, where you feel like everything has aligned itself at a precise moment so that it simultaneously feels both familiar yet engagingly undiscovered. Consequently, they are times in which I could have happily remained in awe and wonder at God; his timing so specific, his knowledge of me so acute, because when the veil lifts, you want to stay on the mountain. But however freely the pieces fall into place, we cannot stay up there and press pause. The most I can do is to cultivate my awareness for the next time I meet him.

So what have I learned from the above? For Emmaus roads to occur along our many ordinary unlit paths, I believe one necessity exists; your life must get to a point where, more than anything else on earth, you need to *want to see God's presence*. We have a choice to interpret moments of encounter as such because seeing requires faith. I would like to finally illustrate this with a third road encounter with Christ from the Bible. It occurred when the Pharisees tried to trap Jesus with a trick question about paying taxes to Caesar under law. Jesus held the loose change, highlighting Caesar's name and engraved face, and responded, 'give back to Caesar what is Caesar's, and to God what is God's.'[14] Earthly power often lies in one face, but divine signature lies in all faces.

When I run the roads of marathons or local Saturday morning Parkruns, I see many faces. They are joyful, hopeful; others are struggling or defeated. They all bear God's image, both the strangers and the friends. I'm aware of them all because running clears other distractions temporarily. My head feels released and I'm more sensitive to the extremes etched upon them, a spectrum ranging from pain to euphoria, especially because I've shared in these emotions. The only other time I have ever experienced such a leveller is in hospital wards, where the pace and random placing of stories and personalities side by side eventually leads to an altered state of seeing.

My point is that I see better on the roads, like a man called Bartimaeus. He was sitting alongside the road, blind and begging, when he heard the people paparazzi that often amassed when Jesus was on the move. Bartimaeus, knowing of Jesus' rumoured potential, cried out for mercy, threw off his coat and approached the voice. When Jesus asked the physically blind Bartimaeus what he wanted for himself, Bartimaeus gave a respectful yet obvious reply, 'Rabbi, I want to see.'[15] The start of an encounter by a roadside, a place of shame fit only for an outcast, a place of waiting. It is as Jesus leaves town that Bartimaeus is seen, shoved to the edge, way down the pecking order, meeting him on the margins.

And it is on the outer edge of society that Jesus says *his* faith has saved and healed him, good news for this underdog as: 'In that very instant he recovered his sight and followed Jesus down the road.'[16] In a second remarkable moment, here Bartimaeus exercises independence of spirit and the luxury of choices: whatever the future had in store for him, physical independence meant he could now have some say in it, and his priority was to track Christ. I think he was hungry to learn, drawn to the magnetic Nazarene. Blind Bartimaeus could now see, therefore a new Bartimaeus followed.

Wanting to see, being granted sight from the margins, then using that new sight. Going deeper, most importantly of all three lessons here, is *why* Bartimaeus wanted sight. He was a beggar whose questions had presumably been for food, clothes or money until this point, a practical request for a basic human need, until a greater need made itself known when he heard 'Jesus of Nazareth [was] passing by'[17] whereupon Jesus' reputation draws a new question out of him. Bartimaeus wanted specifically to see *Jesus*, uniquely, much like I have often hungered for a clearer vision of God himself. There is a parallel here with the Emmaus road and what it means to actually see. I believe that we are all blind until we've seen Jesus and changed our original questions, moving on from a rut of rhetoric where Christ has remained stuck for too long. As independent people of independent spirit, I find that choosing to run enables me to follow him. As I run, he draws from me a new hunger for a vision of God with new questions. I now know that Jesus meets me along the roads.

Back to those two runners in the park, gathering in their familiar Westernised running kit of luminous jackets, compression tights and Nike swooshes catching the early morning light opposite my window. Five minutes after they jog away and I continue typing, a most unexpected sight occurs as a woman in Islamic dress heads along the same path and in the same direction. Black hijab, long full-length black clothes, stunning white trainers with orange trim around the sole, robes swirling but light-footed, like a figure from ancient times joyfully bursting free from history's cage into the present; a resurrection in sport. I didn't expect to see her silhouette jogging through the park; in fact, her pace could quite easily catch them, wherever they are now. I smile at this beautiful running surprise. God nudges me, as if to remind me to open my eyes; to live expectantly; to never close them on grounds of likelihood, cultural stereotypes, disappointments, or even death, but to always remain alert to the arrival of a third person, of him, along Emmaus roads.

4

Out of the Fire

Where can I go from your Spirit? Where can I flee from your presence? . . . If I say, 'Surely the darkness will hide me and the light become night around me,' even the darkness will not be dark to you; the night will shine like the day, for darkness is as light to you.[1]

Running has become a private crucible in which fullness of life seems more pronounced to me, like a radio becoming tuned and when my shoulders begin to relax. This discovery saw me through one of the most significant transitions of my life; that of moving out of paid into unpaid ministry. I use these terms deliberately because I believe this to be the only distinction. If following Jesus, and thereby taking up our place within the church, 'his bride',[2] qualifies us to face outwards in loving all others like the bridegroom does, then ministry is non-selective and will always mean all of us in partnership with God. There really is no difference, we all need each other regardless of our roles within the church, but it is necessary that some are paid leaders because I believe this to be a gift which God gives. Theologically, I know this, but until you move from civic in-fluencer, a centre of your community, to anonymous worker in a non-church setting, you cannot *truly* know it. I got to know it over time which coincided with more running, and I believe that running was my saviour, without which I am not sure that I would have coped.

Before I delve into the opening words of this chapter, I want to tell you about the earliest stages of this transition; the point where one begins to knock on doors of opportunity and utter prayers you never imagined you would. I want to refer to a man from the Old Testament called Abraham who was led by God to climb a mountain in the region of Moriah to make a sacrifice,[3] not the customary sacrifice of a lamb upon burning wood but that of his only son. If fear of God, or sincere respect of him means not withholding that which we love, Abraham proved it. We talk of uphill struggles which require effort or bring discomfort, but I cannot comprehend the confusion of Abraham as he ascended with the knife and Isaac with the woodpile. As a person who thinks in music and pictures, I always come back to Abraham when my running playlist gifts me Kate Bush's 'Running Up That Hill' who, although addressing a very different dilemma of men and women lacking understanding of one another, wrote words about creating agreements with God that enabled their places to be mutually swapped.[4] The story then recounts, however, that God, knowing Abraham's obedience, instructed him not to harm Isaac. Abraham instead used a ram which had been caught by its horns in a nearby thicket, consequently naming that place 'The LORD Will Provide'. The providing of God has become a theme of my unpaid ministry.

When I first travelled down to Kent for my interview for a teaching post, I stopped by at the house of two friends, a married couple who had been my church leaders in London at the time I had met my wife. They were highly experienced Salvation Army Officers, bore the scars of various international ministries but, as I discovered over a welcome cup of tea, clearly retained much wisdom. I recounted my story to them of tiptoeing away from Officership, slightly anxious about their response to my self-imposed exile, only to hear them endorse my climb with this story of Abraham and Isaac. They suggested that perhaps I didn't need to continue with the walk up the hill to perform the sacrifice I had once understood needed making. God knew I held him as my authority because I had not withheld my life's work from him; they assured me that he would now provide. Just as in my meeting at the service station, more encouragement from such friends meant that the blue Tempro line was in good health; God could place people in our lives at a time and place to further our walk with him, however misty the road or steep the ascent.

Earlier on in the journey, there had also been a humorous symbol of 'The LORD Will Provide'. Coming from a lifestyle where all practical needs such as a house and car were provided out of a monthly allowance, purchasing a Fiat Multipla was one small step for a man, but one giant leap for a Salvation Army Officer. Although it never stole the road based upon image, this Italian-designed bubble of a car certainly turned heads because its body shape resembled the foot of an overweight lady squeezing into a high-heeled shoe. I'm no Stig,[5] but I once asked it some questions on a trip to the Lake District, and let me assure you, before you rush out and buy a collector's piece, that the Multipla was not designed for conversation with the road. With a chassis as wide as a tank's, my family never squeezed into it but spread out into this TARDIS[6] across its three seats, front and back. My children were young enough to marvel at their cup holders, which was fortunate because this odd-looking vehicle is all we could afford. It was the first sign of our departure as we began to loosen ties, like a government triggering Article 50 of an unchartered Brexit pathway.

The car experiment was fun and lasted about a year before the Fiat virtually died. Since then, when I see rare Multiplas today, often when out running, I recall how God helped us to face the early vertex of transition. With a smile on my face, I digest these dated experiments in wide design parked in front driveways; collector's pieces ready for a weekend's tinkering, always in need of TLC as much as a successful MOT. Humorously, as we took our first tentative steps, planting a flag into the surface of a new moon, I can now see how the Lord provided.

The bigger issue was changing employment and I was not naïve in this area. Our Salvation Army superiors were faultless to the last, supporting, questioning, listening and endorsing. I was not looking for an easier ride. In practical terms, this step took me out of the frying pan and into the fire and I was fully aware that it could; working longer hours, meeting more deadlines, being more closely managed. With the blisters of Officership still there, I began working as a teacher again (I had worked for four years as head of Art in an independent school), and was officially judged as 'inadequate' at my first lesson observation. Ofsted's brutal choice of vocabulary does nothing for the beginner-teacher (in terms of teaching all subjects in the state sector), and they were tough days. But coming from the vulnerable position of rural church planting (I had sometimes invested hours in preparing church gatherings where virtually nobody turned up), at least I knew my class of thirty would be present each day to engage with my tailored teaching. It must be said, however, that the core congregation of our church plant had been superb supporters and that the vanity was all mine. I must have been raw for attendance arguments to appear legitimate, to trade a calling on such terms, but on one level there was a guarantee to classroom teaching, an audience for my lonely endeavour, some company at last.

Where church leadership had been challenging, teaching brought no sabbatical. Initially, as described, there was pressure from all sides and I was sinking, having chosen to leave a difficult situation only to enter a worse one. The commonly used 'frying pan into the fire' phrase almost fits, but the two terms need to be switched for my own story. The fire is a place of intense heat and light, arguably greater than that of the frying pan. In Salvation Army tradition, much is written about God's presence as the Holy Spirit who is often referred to as 'the fire', alluding to Pentecost.[7] You cannot really escape this theme when the movement's motto is 'blood and fire', using Christ's crucifixion and the Holy Spirit's presence as its emotive foundations. Fire permeates this Army's ethos, so walking away from it was leaving the fire behind; everybody we knew; the familiarity of its subculture; the high expectations of those who cheered us on; the guarantee of success, which God would grant, transmitting from its jingoistic melodies; and our job for life should we choose.

A frying pan, on the other hand, is where raw ingredients are combined, flavours are conjured and seasoning is added; a space for experimentation, where none can be sure what will come of it. Where the fire had been a consuming heat, I now had some control and could adjust things as needed. I don't want this to sound like a struggle for power; in fact, many Officers nowadays have so much input in where and what they do that there has been a monumental power shift over the movement's history from a sending culture to a consultative one. The sending culture had never once bothered me; that was actually part of the fire's appealing, consuming impact. But we were now entering new territory where we had to make choices about how to continue ministry through making friends, going to work, how to achieve a healthy work/life balance, the discovery of Sabbath on a Sunday. (While I appreciate that the day of the week is not key here, it's easy to convince yourself that religious work is Sabbathing and the temptation to do DIY on other days of the week was always too strong to resist.) This last choice brought a dilemma which truly caught me off guard, because when it's been your job to go to church, the change in rhythm felt very heavy to carry.

Entering the frying pan of freedom and choices brought other hidden beliefs to the surface, compounded by necessary shifts away from believing misunderstandings about God. For example, as a child of around primary school age, I used to believe that Jesus was financially loaded, probably due to the kind of songs we sang during the Sunday school offering. As my coppers hit the bottom of that glass jar, I was already opening an account with God who held the financial clout over our lives. Little surprise, then, that I grew to believe that he also held clout when it came to forgiveness too, suspicions which clog the arteries of grace within Christian faith. What a revelation to learn that a man can still be used by God outside of the structures the church creates: 'His love has no limit, his grace has no measure', as one old song says.[8] Thank God that receipt of fullness of life is so much more than finances or banked goodness.

Once again, the only definitive article of our English language also clung to my feet like dust I couldn't shake. Officer employment is referred to as 'the work', just like its vocation being 'the call', elevating it above all other forms of work, which really didn't help my state of mind. The trauma of a changed narrative was akin to breaking one's own heart. A hierarchy of service is opposed to the notion of a priesthood of all believers[9] and works against the equally accessible and knowing reach of

God, as discovered by the writer of the psalm at the start of our chapter. Some terms need thorough examination in light of Scripture before they cause further damage.

But entering the frying pan meant testing this divine reach, and now, ten years later, God is still good to me. I didn't expect it. My *modus operandi* is to analyse and reflect, a Schulz's Charlie Brown[10] of Christianity, flitting between nervousness and optimism, reluctant to truly exercise freedom of choice for fear that something bad may happen when an Officer asserts themselves to leave the glorious fire. But there has been no thunderbolt yet, and I never once regarded three brain haemorrhages and consequent strokes as conspiring to scare me back into it. Some may seek for a message that God is trying to get through to us akin to Job's miserable comforters enforcing their unrequested therapy, but if my left arm could have moved at such suggestions, I might have swung a fist. Generalisations when it comes to the sensitivities and complexities of suffering do not even deserve answers, at least, not in the world I inhabit. If you have ever suffered, you will know this to be true. Instead, for this Chuck there has been a surprising continuation of ministry off the leash and I'm writing this chapter to give you permission too and to let you know that it's OK. Grace is one of the church's best-kept secrets, the unmerited favour of God. The ability to see beauty, to smile, even laugh, to enjoy oneself, to sleep at night, to believe that your life is as valued as the next person's, whichever job you do. When I left the fire, it felt like licking my fingers and pinching this flame. Could grace possibly abound?

Apart from experiencing immense kindness and patience from those I have worked with in the field of education, often reminding me how Christ would minister from the most unexpected of sources, God has brought moments of leadership in the frying pan of the workplace. Looking back, I've had responsibility for the spiritual development and creation of reflective spaces for hundreds of children through worship and teaching in schools; I've had fresh insight into the lives of others, the pressures they face, the hills and valleys of family life, always feeling pastorally drawn towards them; space to form my own conclusions about the way teams work and the way personalities interact, valuing every contribution in the patchwork effort that emerges from a school staff room; to be blessed by headteachers of patience and encouragement; to train others in the field of motivating children to learn, and engaging them in their own emotional and intellectual growth process, all an echo of my own story of leaving the fire. Every moment I stand before a whole school community is now a moment of God's grace.

And people's expectations of the established church have ironically created the possibility for direct use of my theological training outside of the fire. It seems that one doesn't often come across clergy teachers, so I have been privileged to lead a relative's funeral service for one colleague I met along the teaching road, school eucharist services, and am currently working on a wedding. These are redemptive moments. Yes, run-of-the-mill for existing vicars doing their job, but for a teacher wearing hats of experience, a humbling reminder of the trust placed within me, and delightful experience of the enduring goodness of God. To be asked to be involved in such significant times awakens me to a continuing worthiness for ministry, because again, when I entered the frying pan there were no guarantees. So, bizarrely, I have experienced the rare opportunity of being involved in tent-making[11] from two directions: a paid minister working in schools, then a paid teacher leading in churches – a healthy lesson in the fluidity of ministry and God's endorsement upon those who leave the fire and enter the frying pan. It appears that God's activity knows no limits of setting or human-made identity. Could he, in fact, be on our side, always?

Getting closer to awareness of my fragility, I have processed most of this with every breath during running, long running, hours of running. It is evident that one cannot escape the gaze of God, not even by approaching darkness away from fire. When I run in the dark, he is with me; I cannot flee from his presence.[12] Behind this transitional decade of illness, recovery and running, my faith has altered beyond expectation, dare I say to a more resilient, healthy understanding. I now *know* that God is ever present, even in the frying pan.

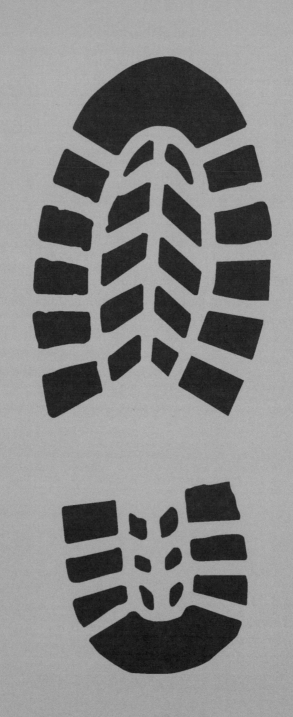

5

Faith (and Fullness of Life)

*The thief comes only to steal and kill and destroy; I have
come that they may have life, and have it to the full.*[1]

The beginnings of faith are a thrilling time. I remember the
urgency, hopefulness and relief to discover that God accepted
me and had 'a plan for my life'. He was not going to ruin it by
taking things away; this was not a reduction but an addition,
an increase to my understanding of what it meant to be fully
human. Too good to be true? This chapter tells how the exhaustion of marathon running has taught me what fullness of
life was *not* intended to mean.

I have an evolving understanding of what it means to live
as a Christian, and my early days compare very differently
with today. This is probably because we runners spend a lot
of time out there on the road, mulling things over, inside our
own heads. I mostly run with an old iPod and headphones for
company and have found some great friends via Apple's iTunes
over the years, in particular the late Haddon Robinson – a
gravelly, sandpaper-voiced preacher with a rich New York accent, Ravi Zacharias – an apologist of international reputation
who came to faith after the crisis of trying to take his own life,
and more recently Revd Dr Samuel Wells – vicar of St Martin-
in-the-Fields, London. Their voices have become my 'running
buddies' because I mostly run alone, yet with their thoughts

and beautifully crafted teaching I never *feel* alone. In fact, it's strange how an intellectually stimulating podcast can get you up a hill as well as a hit by Stevie Wonder; the brain responds and somehow fuels the next step. Or perhaps it's because I'm reassured by their articulation of God in Christ, a suffering God, which breathes life into my own aching body.

Either way, running has shown faith to be an act of discipline and endurance, a far cry from the commencement of my Christian experience when the Holy Spirit energised my life with a sense of hope that I had never known and I expected the road to be a love-filled breeze. My conversion was a dramatic turnaround, and all from reading a pamphlet called *Why Jesus?* as I noted earlier, written by Nicky Gumbel of Holy Trinity Church, Brompton, London. After that night, sat alone on my bed, I was going to convert all England with my arguments for the truth of Christ, such was my evangelical energy; I didn't want to sleep, just run with words of argument because I had found the blue line. Prayers seemed to be answered by first-class post, a predictable exchange like an order from Amazon. Jesus had come to bring fullness of life[2] and mine was now overflowing with a meta-narrative that would never run dry. At least that was the early days, but nothing stays the same forever and we can't survive on baby food or childish ways; bad things happen, so the blue line became fainter as the road went on.

There is a difference between having *a full life* and experiencing the fullness *of* life as promised by Jesus. We can have diaries of scheduled good things, be on as many church rotas as humanly possible, yet still lack it. Unfortunately, much of Christianity today attracts newcomers with the seduction of maximum experience, a sense of personal significance and history-making, the promise of a life lived in HD. Sure, these things could well be a by-product of faith in Christ, but this is a skewed, biased gospel, like misrepresented water that is offered only as 'wet'. Water is so much more; it flows, it transfers, it hydro-powers, even transports, it sustains physical bodies because it hydrates and therefore gives life. I appreciate it even more now I'm a runner. I believe that the cross of Christ similarly has more dimensions than making me happy or significant. I want to take you for a moment beyond the attractional gospel of Jesus as some kind of superhero who makes people feel good, and look deeper into a fullness of life where the template lies in this cross. It involves inconvenience, countercultural to a Western world of comfort and immediacy. It may cause you to reflect, as opposed to guaranteed success. It may ask you to have faith instead of certainty.

Inconvenience and reflection are common features of a distance runner's life, so it seems best to illustrate fullness of life (and what it's not) with a one city tale of two marathons – London in 2012 and 1998. Fourteen years after my first attempt, 2012 should have been a slower run on paper, but in this year of the London Olympics, experience was king. I had trained to run all the way, no walking, building up endurance over six months, following the rhythm the magazines advise; gradually increasing time on my feet over the winter, rest days, increasing mileage as daylight increased in the new year, rehearsing hydration strategies, building up the miles towards March before loving the reduction of 'the taper' in order to take my place confidently on the starting line. Of course, every amateur runner knows that success in a marathon is reaching the starting line injury-free, not just completing the course. And I arrived there, feeling like a tightly wound spring, with a quiet belief that I was going to run it all the way round today.

I did what I always do on race days; arrived early, sat on a park bench, rehearsed my timing splits and people-watched. Anything under five hours, with stops to hug friends and family, would be a good day. I know there are much faster runners out there but I just wanted to run the whole distance. After one more listen to Queen's *Radio Ga Ga* and being transported in my imagination to those cold, rainy nights jogging through the rain around my community in Ashford, I felt ready to head to the military operation of the fleet of huge lorries that are baggage check-in.

The starting pen is always surrounded by crash barriers. I could feel the bounce in a pair of new socks and spongey Adidas trainers beneath me. I would not normally have chosen bright blue and green for trainers, but after the gait analysis it was Adidas's season shoe for my size and budget. (At the time I wondered if the colour would even make me run faster because I wouldn't want to be recognised!) Looking around at the vests and T-shirts of charities, some printed with personal messages, it was clear that there were thousands of reasons to take place in the largest fundraising event on the planet. There was a buzz in the air as we waited for the start, and I got chatting to a guy running for Hope HIV,[3] a charity for AIDS orphans in Africa whose founder I happened to know. Small world, long race – the siren sounded.

It took ages to get running, the dense field walking and laughing, then jogging for a few seconds, then walking again. Finally, after what seemed like fifteen minutes, we were off and I started my Garmin with its reassuring beep as I passed under the official race clock. It was still congested and I could not get into my race pace. Some runners hopped onto the pavement for more room, weaving in and out of the residents of houses close by, some of whom had chosen to remain inside their garden gates with children leaning forwards for high-fives. Anxious to save energy, I got around this dilemma by carrying a water bottle in my left hand, but oddly for the first mile I just could not feel my legs. Runners always say 'never trust the first mile', but my legs were shaking and I put it down to nerves. I had spent the previous night sleeping on a friend's floor but had literally got zero hours sleep. I'd tried everything from counting sheep to imagining Arsenal's offside trap repeatedly halting football matches in the 1980s, but the later it got the more anxious I became until this was replaced by excitement and the chirping of birds outside. Perhaps my legs were now telling me something?

I raced on and eventually the feeling subsided and I began to recognise my running rhythm. It felt so familiar, so enjoyable, I was on top of the world, high on running. I remember well-wishers shouting my name, and it felt so good to be back running London. Around mile 6, I was overtaken by a man dressed as the Blackpool Tower who was understandably taking all the cheers of the crowd. I thought, 'How did he train? Do costumed record-breaking runners have to sneak out in the middle of the night dressed as exotic zoo creatures or carrying fridge freezers? Outside of a stag night, it can't be easy explaining to the police why you are dressed pretending to ride an ostrich at 2 a.m.'

The crowds grew deeper as we headed towards the first real wall of sound, Greenwich and the Cutty Sark. When the crowd noise hits, you feel very special, like a movie star striding a red carpet. We runners are the reason they are here, but they have gone through this training period with its ups and downs too, bored by our talk of recovery drink flavours, Saturday afternoons collapsed on the sofa following a 20-mile run and developing preferences in compression clothing. I slowed to almost a trot as I had arranged to meet my wife and children near this landmark. I scaled the crowd desperately searching for their faces and had almost given up when ahead of me I saw a cardboard sign, 'Go Ozzie, Go!' That's my nickname, and I pulled over and hugged my own tribe. I showed them the back of my vest with the surprise message thanking them for their support, before running off into the distance. My running journey has been much theirs too; I wouldn't have come this far today without them.

Having seen my family, I was now able to relax into my running, feeling very comfortable throughout and taking in London's wonderful atmosphere and the mass rhythm of the spectrum of vests ahead of me. Marathon days are truly some of the best days of my life: the goodwill amongst the crowd, the single intention of the runners to finish, the unity of purpose and encouragement between these parties – it feels much like a wedding day. My pace and hydration strategies all went as planned, and apart from losing a satellite signal briefly underneath some darker bridges around Docklands, with my Garmin to guide me I felt in control the whole way round, finally finishing in four hours fifty-two with arms raised along The Mall. A textbook 'no walking and get round' marathon.

If only fullness of life was like this – predictable, on track, reciprocal. But it's not, and my 1998 marathon provides a more realistic illustration of the life of faith. Losing my GPS signal had made me panic slightly in 2012, leading my brain to reflect upon prayers for guidance in my life where I had felt I had lost all connection with God, but in '98 I was naïve and completely unprepared for the journey of a marathon. I had signed up for a faster finishing time of around four hours, then realised on the day that I was penned in at the start with lots of club runners wearing 'Sub 4'[4] merchandise (Sub 4 carries a bit of kudos amongst runners). I just trusted youth – I had done some training but picked up chickenpox in the February – so began very cautiously and without any pacing watch, but before long was running all alone and feeling a little left behind. Eventually running a fast middle third as I passed some runners who had left me at the start, I was learning the hard way that dependency on self and schoolboy reputations were an arrogant mistake.

It was at mile 19 where I began to think the unthinkable for a closet-competitive runner like me – should I just walk? My brain began to misfire, the mental jostling in my head would not subside, miles began to feel much longer than I remembered them from training and I was shutting down. My training had been quite basic and mind-numbingly boring, before the days of GPS and iPods in my life, so I just ran in silence and ran how I felt, repeating 4-mile laps of my parents' neighbourhood. I would pass a greengrocer's on each lap and increasingly desire to steal bananas displayed outside the front, but never did. I had bought some Asics Gel trainers and managed to run in them for a few weeks before the race, marvelling at the technology of running on a gel cushion responding to the pressure of my heel and toe movement. But at mile 19 there were no bananas and even the Asics were no longer my friend. I hit the dreaded 'wall'.

I had heard of the wall but invincible youth had convinced me it would never come my way. It is the moment when glycogen (carbohydrate stored in the body for energy) becomes depleted and feelings of fatigue and negativity become overwhelming, and I could not even count any more. At that moment, I hated running, I hated everything; my body had let me down and the script I had written for myself as a successful first-time marathon runner was ripped away from me. I resented the sound of each breath of runners passing me close by, looking comfortable, and felt embarrassed as a walker which was new territory for a proud athlete like me. I could hardly make out the blue line, looking down at my feet, just finding the energy for the next step of staggered walking. Dehydrated and disillusioned, an elderly lady in the crowd must have read my red face because she leaned forward with a handful of fun-sized Mars bars and I grabbed one. I nibbled the chocolate off first, all the way round like a child on a school trip who needs to make it last the whole journey, before downing the rectangular blob that remained. A chewy rush and almost immediately belief returned – I could run again.

I finished the race jogging the last 6 miles, before finding a sprint in front of Buckingham Palace – 'Where did that come from? Couldn't I have used that further back?' I thought. Medal and photograph followed, but not the memory I had hoped for. It was made worse by looking for my name amongst the finishers in *The Times* newspaper the following week. Day 1 no name, day 2 no name, and so on until Friday when I made it. Hardly the headline I had imagined, and a wake-up call for somebody with a false self-image and much to learn about endurance running.

As I write these memories, I can see how distance running always provides me with a faith lesson and an absolutely necessary bringing down to size. The contrast between the two marathons also speaks to me of two opposing messages about fullness of life and clarifies for me what Jesus did *not* promise to the faithful. While 1998 was disastrous on a physical level, it was a revelation on a spiritual one – perhaps God is not most interested in the easy life? Perhaps the twists and turns are a necessary part of it? Maybe I needed to see who I really was? 2012 felt successful but was without incident and disappointment, therefore resembling less a true reflection of the real faith lived in the real world that I have spent the past twenty-five years coming to know.

I set out to write an honest book, and looking in the mirror as a runner, I have to admit to the conclusion that because I have hit something of a wall in faith terms, fullness of life is no longer the guarantee of a happy, healthy innings consisting of heroic deeds for God; It must be *better than that*, there must be more to it. It is not a cheap exchange, otherwise people would only believe in God for what he could bring them – hardly the love of a free will, and churches would be bulging at the seams with people seeking their superhero biography in Christ's name (you may have noticed, however, that some Christian songs today veer in this direction and leaders of musical worship need great discernment in this area).

Instead, faith and fullness of life must mean accepting that God creates at great risk, almost wastefully, allowing us to freely run the races of our lives. His abundant human existence (through which God's reign known as 'the kingdom of God' was present before us) was eventually so threatening that it aroused destructive choices in others. But Christ's life of love could not be extinguished upon the cross, from which point death, devoid of its sting, was defeated,[5] bringing life to people like me who no longer need to fear it. In part, fullness of life means the freedom to live as Jesus lived, a beckoning to welcome others into our lives regardless of the cost, and any definition outside of this falls short.

Fullness of life, therefore, also knows that the joy of resurrection was not constrained by circumstances, Jesus' apparent
failure, but made possible *through them*. Therefore, the church
does not need to be embarrassed by suffering, sweeping it under the carpet to present a fullness of life-giving God. In my
life, God leaves suffering out in the open, brutally obvious, like
meat attracting flies as inadequate explanations stack up. By
doing this, he asks me to believe that each time, it can be taken
and transformed through the power of his resurrection and it
is these Mars bar moments that enable faith development to
take place.

If you are going to live this full life, you will need other
people. A privilege of my life has been the pace-setters who
have come alongside me; men who are not necessarily runners,
but who give me a model, enable me to raise my effective-
ness and draw the best out of me. Their experience reminds
me how to live with poise and a sense of humour once in a
while. Peter Hodgson is a great friend, an Anglican Reader in
his eighties who has pretty much seen it all, church-wise, pas-
toring people for years and becoming a figure in his Yorkshire
community with the gravitas of George Lucas's Yoda. He writes
that 'the real Christian attitude to suffering – the real Christian
acceptance – is not just to take it in humble resignation, but
to take it on! Believing in the fundamental goodness of life
because of the resurrection of Christ, I will take this chaotic,
meaningless raw material and I will fashion it and make use
of it. There are numerous possibilities'.[6] Peter's creative link
bridges Jesus' cry of abandonment and his announcement that
'It is finished'.[7] This sounds like a fuller life to me. God was in
the cross of Christ modelling the creative exchange necessary
for a more abundant life, good news for a human race who

often hit the wall. Let's not build problematic faith walls for ourselves by running from this difficult exchange; let's run towards it and take it on.

Fullness of life for you could be about changed expectations; to live with God's rhythms and to work at Jesus' offer, sometimes leaving behind the conventions everybody else believes. For example, it fascinates me how Jesus' healing encounters didn't linger; some people returned to follow him while others didn't. While blind Bartimaeus did, only one of the ten lepers chose to do so,[8] and apparently Jesus left this one in ten conversion ratio as a loose end. These unclosed parentheses indicate that healing was only part of what he could bring, providing a glimpse into a fuller life in one sense but not the whole. Jesus must consequently have a broader vision for completeness in the human condition than simply not being ill. Samuel Wells's sermon 'Does God Heal?'[9] is a masterpiece I wholeheartedly recommend; it hides from nothing and is a transparent examination of this subject in greater depth than here. He says so much more in fewer words, but my hunch is that we don't want to put in the time-consuming work to mine deeply into fullness of life beyond the spectacular and immediate. Without Wells's broad definition of salvation as a glorious trilogy revealing God's desire for humanity, where freedom from past guilts or hurts and hope for the future sandwich themselves around the present, I don't see how we can still look one another straight in the eye on this matter of healing. Yes, physical healing occurred then and sometimes does now, but should it not, the consistency of God's character as one of love and presence is not a gaping wound in my faith. I still trust him.

If this is making you think guilty thoughts, James Fowler's *Stages of Faith* refers to maintaining the status quo as the

'Synthetic-Conventional Stage'[10] at which religious institutions work best. Rebranding fullness of life may feel counter to the church's desire in some places, but self-governance requires a willingness to interrupt our reliance upon external authority. This moves towards Fowler's Stage 4, with an 'Individual-Reflective Faith'[11] which has worked its way into my life due to the solitude of running and the illness of three strokes. Perhaps this is your time to move on?

In my experience, fullness of life is not an abundance of material things, nor was Jesus presented as wealthy. Jesus does not try to attract followers with a universal message of health, prosperity or length of days, just knowing 'the only true God, and Jesus Christ, whom you have sent'.[12] This kind of fullness of life is beyond what we might anticipate or even think we need sometimes; it is a spiritual abundance which incorporates a process of falling, recovering and enduring, releasing us from misguided expectations around difficult times in life, or in runner's terms, confronting 'the wall'. Hitting it dumped me at the end of my resources in 1998. It was a reluctant, painful surrender. I hit it hard as a first-time marathon runner and as a believer later on, once I was in church leadership ministry.

Perhaps I should have seen this spiritual wall coming in Bible college? On the surface I was living with other resident students of a similar mind, but simplicity and the wider good of the community were not always my highest priority. Personally, I never pushed through to a more demanding selfless life, or the disciplines of a monastic dedication (living behind the brickwork boundary of the austere William Booth College) spiritually or materially, but do not blame anyone else for my choices. Perhaps I should have again seen it coming in Officer ministry? The lifestyle never sat comfortably; serving the needy but returning to my plenty caused friction within my faith. Of course, each circumstance is different, but with a volunteer's allowance (Officers are not regarded as employees) which benefited me with the option of a larger television or the latest technology, it seemed a tricky circle to square and was a personal angst. Of course, stewardship is challenging for all Christians, whether leaders or not, but being a runner, I probably have an extremist streak and am not averse to personal discipline, so the pieces didn't quite hang together.

Like the returning prodigal son, my church ministry had to get to the point of emptiness before I could know the running Father's unmerited welcome, known as grace. The sharp truth is that faith in God and experience of fullness of life has no room for personalities. As Oswald Chambers writes, 'Undress yourself morally before God of everything that might be a possession until you are a mere conscious human being, and then give God that.'[13] I thank God that the exhaustion of marathon running has helped me to see this more clearly and to know the truth about fullness of life.

6

Blisters

Just then a woman who had been subject to bleeding for twelve years came up behind [Jesus] and touched the edge of his cloak.[1]

Whatever positive spin we choose to put upon a life of following Jesus and our touching distance from supernatural power, we cannot pretend that we do not live in a world where suffering exists and its effects are real. Whether we are its recipients or its cause, it is with us. For all the stories of answered prayer and the evidenced power of God (as experienced by the woman in the above story from the New Testament), we can think of equal accounts where people have died and God seems to have fallen silent, or where we have said the wrong thing and only made matters worse. In my opinion, church can sometimes be rather queasy over the touching distance of suffering. It shows our falling into temptation to keep our suspicion of a disinterested God out of sight in our desire to make him attractive to others, either because our church culture disapproves, or because we are only expected to be evangelical about the good times. Not many churches support people in coping with unanswered prayers of faith, teach about it, or spend time wrestling with the reality of a silent God within decision-heavy lifestyles, but looking ahead, surely blister rhetoric could become more evangelical than the forgery.

Courtship of the make-me-happy God has manifested itself in many ways during my life, but in particular the isolation of Bible verses such as the favourite, '"For I know the plans I have for you," declares the LORD, "plans to prosper you and not to harm you, plans to give you hope and a future",'[2] tugged from its original context to decorate everything from banners to bookmarks. This often isolated verse portrays a far deeper, more resilient hope that rings true alongside my own journey. In the opening to his *Divine Conspiracy*,[3] Dallas Willard talked about the seduction of things which are partly true, statements which can draw you in to such an extent that you place a mental full stop after them. But blisters move you into new ways of seeing, like a necessary three-step process from initial conversion to discipleship then again to a new conversion. It has happened as I have aged too, moving from unknowns to guarantees at conversion, then on to peace with the emerging unknowns today. Dare I say that I even *like* the unknowns now?

The misread prophet Jeremiah was writing to a people exiled from Jerusalem to Babylon, and he had a sense that God wanted them to seek the prosperity of their new surroundings, to dig in for the long haul, to invest in it by planting gardens, building houses and making it better. If they can only live in the present instead of being mentally overwhelmed with their future, this will prove their trust in God. This is not the easy option, but shows how God works through the blister of wishing things to be different to what they are. It is also a promise to a community, never an individual, and is miles from being intended as words to propel anyone towards individualised fame, leaving God in brackets. What comfort there is to be gained from a proper reading here, where God knows where we are on the map, doesn't want us to panic and will move through the blisters with us.

I don't want to spend my life tiptoeing around the blisters caused by geographical, emotional or relational exile, never fully living. For God to be consistent, therefore, it comes down to the type of God one holds onto during exile. If he is only good because he physically heals, I can find you plenty of bemused Christians who stick with him through disappointment and unanswered mail. Perhaps it is only they who know what faith means, when reason and intellect have shed their last flicker of light? We know that God neither stops nor pre-empts suffering to give us prosperity and hope, the snakes on the board game of Jeremiah's misrepresented promise, but in Christ, he demonstrated that they need not have the last word. In illness I have found that it is through the shadow of mortality, a full stop approaching before it is due, that a deadline actually improves efficiency as we experience a new flourishing and healthy nudge that we, too, are fully human.

Mining this biblical promise gives deeper truth. Blisters in a Christian life mean that I reach out for anything of Christ, like the bleeding woman, clinging to an edge of God's consistent power to save the story in ways that I cannot imagine. With creativity that surpasses mine, the crucified then resurrected Christ is the game-changer concerning illness. It feels appropriate to mention that there once lived a French Jewess named Simone Weil, dying aged 35, who is buried in my town of Ashford. She said that to cope with any affliction meant going beyond self and thought to Christ, who was the truth, and continued to be so even in his suffering.[4]

But most of us probably aren't at the point of my fellow Ashfordian, so let's bring this all back to where we are and our tentative attempts to make sense of things. Like every runner will tell you, blisters, however small, cannot be ignored because upon them we place our weight and, with each step into the future, are reminded of pain. In my life, barely a week goes by without a news headline or personal story which makes me question, 'OK, God, where are you in this?' I've just watched a televised Notre Dame almost burn to the ground and hundreds kneeling along the banks of the Seine, asking the same question. As I sit in Sunday church behind a person barely able to speak, week after week, does anyone else notice the contradiction between reality and the branded 'fullness of life' where everything is fully fixed and working to its potential, bringing glory to God? Do they not suffer this blister too?

When I started running for more than a bus, I soon became aware of the fear of blisters. I say 'fear' because while I have been fortunate and not really experienced this occupational hazard, running magazines would often give advice about how to avoid them and specialist equipment such as socks are now sold on the basis of seamless technology protecting against them. I have only truly felt the annoyance of blisters from my long primary school holidays riding my BMX around the streets of Ilford, where my hands would suffer from the grips on my handlebars before becoming as calloused as my dad's leather gardening gloves hanging in the shed close by. I learned through this pain that repetitive pressure on one part of my hands or ineffective protection would result in blisters, but of course, as a child I just kept doing it, until the school term recommenced when I recovered as I found instead a new joy in the fingertip navigation of a new pencil case containing an enticing Coca-Cola-scented eraser that I just had to smell.

So it transpired in my early years of belief that overreliance upon one element of Jesus, for example the expectation of a constantly miracle-working hero, would bring me pain; I needed to adjust my grip or change my equipment – which in my case meant scenting a new trail on this captivating man. As a runner, keeping going is always my aim, in spite of emotional pain, physical discomfort or mental tussles with God, but it's not always easy.

I walk past a modern postbox on my commute to work, where the back is transparent so that, once swallowed through its glossy red slot, you see a mounting pile of letters slowly build up throughout the day. These letters always remind me of my prayers, making me question whether they were received. Did they reach their divine destination, or like those letters, do my innermost dreams simply lie in a cascading heap of posted prayers, forgotten, unopened? Unanswered prayer can become a blister if you place all your weight upon immediacy.

In all honesty, I used to operate in peaks and troughs of all-out God insurance; Sundays and church leadership would require me to do so. But my experience of suffering, especially when seizures were frequent, has made me far more reflective, in a respectful way, of applying too much reliance upon the power of a pain-fixing God – who as Scripture records, in Jesus truly healed those with illnesses, including seizures[5] – and simultaneously carrying the guilt of not being faithful enough. At the moment, my symptomatic epilepsy is controlled by a heavy dose of a drug called Keppra twice a day; medicine in the hands of experts has halted its terrifying control, until which point it was not, after prayer and what I had thought was faith, miraculously removed. I never once considered sulking about this; Jesus remained wholly able and good. But I am prepared to let the dilemma lie and believe that the miracle can be found in the control of seizures by medicine and the years of study, expertise and creativity with which God has gifted some.

You will probably ask – is this yet another easy route out? A rather cheap Tempro line to follow? Am I not being faithful enough, like a child with a straightforward faith in a God who longs to be known by intimate terms such as '*Abba*, Father'?[6] Am I, even after all the surgery and fear, still the searching prodigal, needing to come to my senses that my sonship means that God answers every healing prayer? Well, if you are always looking for obvious non-negotiable signs, frankly – he doesn't work that way, he doesn't always give them, so this cannot form part of any blue line. But the magician-not-showing-up is not the last word on blisters. My resilience is anchored in a foundational understanding of a consistently good God, but not a God who amazes me personally with spectacular wonders and quick healings; I don't look to him in that way. Perhaps this is because he knows how changeable I can be, how changeable we can all be, one moment certain – the next analytical. Maybe I would praise him for a day or two were I to be miraculously healed, then return to a state of apathy and reflection over those who aren't, struggling with the injustice of it all and the apparent lottery of divine goodness?

I remember feeling this blister of the random intervention of God acutely in 1994, the most significant year of my life. It was the year my Christian experience truly got off the ground, the year in which I met my wife and also the year of the genocide in Rwanda. I was ignorant at the time of any current affairs outside of the repetitively upbeat small world in which I lived, particularly the 100 days during which 800,000 members of the minority Tutsi community and their political opponents were slaughtered by Hutu extremists. As they murdered in Africa, I was loving in England (actually, learning the choice of love), and it was only when I watched the film *Shooting Dogs*[7] some years later that I appreciated the dichotomy of that time. The dilemma of the Belgian, French and UN peacekeepers presented an unimaginable moral maze, yet it was the Catholic priest, played by the late John Hurt, who represented consistency and the unwavering belief that God was to be found in the centre of the suffering of the Tutsis.

I think this was my first epiphany of what it meant to be incarnational, and I was drawn towards this kind of God; one who showed not the slightest sign of erasing complicated causes of suffering but who chose to transform outcomes by entering into suffering's midst. As I looked back on this significantly good year of my life, it seemed impossible that such extremes could take place on this single earth, spinning silently in space, on one side having its heart ripped out through ethnic atrocities while on mine, my heart was being enlarged. It was a painful lesson, less about God's intervention and more about the availability of grace, learning that God was not the midfield general, spraying passes, controlling the universal ball in the manner I had first hoped. If you think he has dominance, the pain inflicted by one Rwandan upon another and the pain I cause within my sphere of influence today, are evidence enough that *cooperation* with grace is the key. Doing nothing and hoping that God will always bring about change without us, is a blister which I hope eventually arrives in your shoe (if it hasn't done so already).

The grace of God reveals that consistency lies in him and not us, rather like the presence of the sun, ever present in its frosty December dawn light but not always burning me physically with its August intensity. Like the blue line which guides every mentally anguished marathon runner through London's winding streets, following a silent, seemingly absent God who I cannot always feel and who asks more of me than I would like to deal with, to wrestle with and eventually come to terms with, it's a long and difficult road you won't hear preached very often. If only we were more honest about his occasional hiddenness as we share our stories with those who don't yet believe. Accepting that this silent grace is part of his consistency would guard us from walking away from him so quickly when life seems to turn against us; just because it's tough doesn't mean that it is not life in its fullness. His grace, not our works,[8] is how we get through – a trust in his ever-present knowledge of me and my circumstances – sometimes loud whilst other times silent in our noise-filled lives.

There have been other times in my life, apart from running, where I have learned this truth. I am not a great flier, in fact I'm probably the only person to have ever flown from London to Hong Kong without a wink of sleep so that I could keep tabs on the pitch of the engine, the state of the wings and inform the pilot of any minor changes. But fear aside, when I have flown in planes, I am always amazed at how one can take off from a wet and windy Britain then pass through a layer of cloud before emerging above the cotton-wool blanket to realise a clear blue sky and golden sunlight. I am calmed by the blue vastness and peaceful curve of the earth from my window, with the onset of its Polaroid palette out of one side of the aircraft as we end one day or greet another. As with real life and trusting God, rain clouds and storms may temporarily obscure the sun, but I do not doubt its presence.

The blister we feel during hard times is to assume either that an omnipresent God has removed his presence or that we should just be praying for a dramatic breakthrough. Actual tangible 'weather prayers' from believers have always felt ridiculous to my mind; we pray for a hot day for our trip to the beach, while farmers do the opposite for a parched crop amidst a bleak forecast upon their livelihoods. Sunbathers worship a slowly heating planet, while hours away others die from famine. At the root of this lies selfishness, a blind spot often masquerading as a devout prayer life. In fact, we have little excuse for turning a blind eye to our awareness of worldwide needs by comfort eating on the parts of religion that enable us to ignore, for example, the geographical disasters we now see due to the impact of climate change. Often the solution starts with me.

Once again I need saving from myself, from a blister; the distant God I had boxed and I would publicly summon to change the world obviously wants to begin with my habits: with my endeavour to wrap my Christianity in cotton wool and live a longer, healthier life whilst quietly harbouring the doubts, questions, fears and sleepless nights that taint this fullness of life. He wants me to push outwards, to fly freely as a kite, to move on and most importantly, *to enjoy it*. Shockingly simple, but such a miracle may be the only way I can live with both ends of suffering – the pain I receive and that which I give; the agony I recognise and that I will never know, which is symptomatic of the disconnect between not just myself and the world, but my disconnection between image and the true me. This liberation would be real healing for me, and running is generally the time when I am most aware and seek forgiveness over such blisters.

You have probably gathered that I have got a lot wrong in my Christian life, in my private angst about God and the world, and this chapter may have started to sound rather negative. I have made many mistakes, probably just like you, and the theological tussles, the politics of church and the desire to be more Christlike yet meeting the same challenges again and again, like a fly hitting the same pane of glass in its bid for freedom, have sometimes made me want to walk away from Christianity. But I'm a marathon runner, remember, and marathon runners don't quit. I'm a runner who's had three strokes and I run simply because I know the joy of my left arm and leg working in unison. I'm a resigned church leader who has known the grace of God since paid ministry, and there's no way I'm narrowing my vision of him now. These blisters aren't a reason to stop running, so if you know some of them too, this is your time to raise your head for once and make the choice to keep running.

I have been writing much of this chapter while on holiday on the south coast of Pembrokeshire. The other morning I ran a 5k beside the sea; it was very windy, the waves were crashing against the rocks and despite working my arms, I could hardly gain any momentum. Passing a rare dog-walker, I pretended I was enjoying it before taking on the very steep hill that led back to the holiday home as the rest of the family were just rousing from their sleep, surrounded by duvets as undulating as the Welsh hills within which our accommodation was nestled.

A place of beautiful golden beaches, two are joined by a tunnel which plummets you into pitch-black darkness, where you cannot even see the ground underneath your feet because your eyes lack time to adjust. As I was midway through the tunnel, all was calm, there was no sound of wind and I could have remained there in shelter, except it was not a place for staying still. I could feel the drips of water coming through the above rocks, but I could not see anything in this narrow passageway that was built to continue the route of the flat coastal path. I had a choice, almost like those moments in life where you know you need to leave a bad situation behind but lack the courage to move beyond it, but keeping going I burst out the other side 30 seconds later into the buffeting headwind and rain lashing against my cold arms. We cannot become static if we are to know fullness of life or allow the conditions to mould us to choose safety over faith, even safety over exile. Keep running, stay present and you will hear, see or touch something of God, even just an edge.

And here's an edge. I'm a Christian honest enough to confess that some people (who wouldn't call themselves Christian) make a better job of life in all its fullness than I do, through their approach to each day, their love for others and the simple fulfilment of their lives through unquestioning acts requiring neither acknowledgement nor wider meaning. Of course, they have blisters too, but they choose not to broadcast them to the detriment of today. It is at this point that I want to respect one of the most 'free' runners I know. This chapter could easily have remained a shopping list of the problems I've encountered with blisters, but because of another runner, I have found hope through a frayed edge. So, before we move on to chapters exploring the themes of hope and love, I spy the end of the tunnel for my faith-blisters through a particularly mature pace-setter named Edwin Bartlett.

Involvement in the running community has led me towards many people of fitness. Fit runners become people of big hearts physically, but stewarding at my local Ashford Parkrun has brought about my friendship with Edwin; someone with

a non-confrontational, big heart for his home town. He challenges me by his selfless behaviour and several years invested in
making community happen for others. He is, like me, a closet
extremist, but understated (not like me). Reliably involved in
setting up the course every Saturday for the past 250 plus weeks
of the past five years, come snow or rain, Edwin represents silent consistency. He is sort of everything that I'm not; humble,
content to train up and down the same monotonous street if
it's the only patch of road untouched by snow, and a self-styled
'old codger'.[9] Running on average 1,200 miles per year in a
shameless retro running vest and shorts, Edwin started at the
age of 37 before catching the running bug and now defies 75.
Although he 'could run for ever', realistically he will stop four
years from now and give up running after passing forty years,
then take his place as a steward at running events, not because
he wants to give anything back to running but because 'I just
enjoy it'. His simple answer bothers me, forever the analyst,
and I have always been suspicious of pleasure for its own sake,
but Edwin has a peace about his life and I have so much to
learn from him.

Edwin has great stories to tell and makes me laugh as we
walk together on one of our dawn set-ups during winter. He re-
lays the challenge he experienced in eliminating a huge puddle
on the Parkrun course which caused the route to be diverted
to an alternative 'wet course' during the winter season, so he
cleared the drain himself. One night, under cover of darkness,
he also came to the park with a spade, dug a tiny ditch and improved drainage for every Saturday morning's run since. Edwin
is Parkrun's Banksy; he knows where to place kilometre markers via small white marks painted on the park's pathways and
recruits me for a bush-trimming operation the following day

so that we can make the route wider for runners by uncovering the overgrown cycle lane. I'm tired, familiar with church initiatives created to serve the community, but as sidekick to this inspirational pensioner, all the time I'm thinking 'he does this just because he enjoys it'. It's authentic, his life's obsession, and deeply disturbing to a chameleon Christian.

Together we pull the trolley of luminous arrows, traffic cones and kilometre marker signs (which Edwin has loaded with screwdrivers and hooks for special 'secret' attachments to lamp posts) around Victoria Park. I press him repeatedly but he doesn't share about life-blisters of any description. He didn't spend Christmas Day with anyone; he wasn't bothered. He keeps things very simple, showing me his new stopwatch which allows him to continue to 'do the best he can' but acknowledging the mental and physical benefits of running 'just to delay the decay'. Runners are obsessed with timings and my Garmin watch is like a running buddy to me – I can feel quite alone without it. He teaches me about marathons, emphasising the need for a quick start in London while it is flat 'otherwise you get behind the masses and you cannot run fast'. What I glean most from Edwin is that running brings life. He is living proof of the research into longevity through regular physical exercise by Ralph S. Paffenbarger Jr, an epidemiologist, who said that exercise did not just add years to our lives, but life to our years.[10] The most youthful of 75-year-olds, just watching and listening to Edwin and his little pieces of acquired wisdom is a sacred time for me, a moment of grace in the early morning darkness.

When I ran a 10k with Mo Farah (I say 'with' – he was present at the starting line but because of crowds of hundreds I could get nowhere near him), his gazelle-like stride and dark shades left me for dust. This chapter's opening words recalled a haemorrhaging woman's passion to get closer to Jesus, the healing encounter behind Sam Cooke's Soul Stirrers' gospel song entitled 'Touch the Hem of His Garment';[11] I know what it's like to try getting closer. My wife mocks my Edwin-time, my admiration for the simplicity of his outlook, telling me that I am only seeking to touch the edge of his Garmin, but there's more to it than that. He knows that I'm writing a book and is content to be mentioned in it, but has little idea of his powerful example of fullness of life. Exposing my contribution to a world of pain, that I create as much as that which I feel, friendship with Edwin has brought me within touching distance of light at the end of the tunnel when it comes to blisters.

7

Hope (Through Illness)

Let us throw off everything that hinders and the sin that so easily entangles. And let us run with perseverance the race marked out for us.[1]

There is a pendulum to sickness and sometimes it can feel that Christian hope, which offers us a supernatural lifeline, only makes matters worse. This issue can polarise; we may offer comments such as: 'Perhaps God is trying to tell you something' to which another may respond, 'Well, I sure wish he'd written us a letter!' I believe God has written, and it comes in various quotes throughout this book from the apostle Paul's letters, addressed to people in need of encouragement or guidance, such as the opening sentence above on the issue of hindrance. I once heard that faith is forged on the anvil of suffering,[2] and we often read of Jesus' healings accompanied by a comment upon people's faith in him. It follows that to live without suffering could well hinder our development, just like a runner needs to work muscles in developing stamina.

There is, of course, the aspect of our blue line that God still heals today – sometimes, an option which keeps the instant-hope door ajar. But long-term, hope can only be so if we seek an altered future, more specifically an altered self, or as I've already suggested, a fuller, more spiritually abundant life, possible *within* present circumstances. I recently had the opportunity of sharing a coffee with an Olympian, Ian Richards, who represented Great Britain in the 1980 Summer Olympics in Moscow, finishing eleventh in the men's 50km race walk. Ian shares a Christian hope after discovering a Salvation Army church where people 'had an inner sense of contentment which they didn't deserve. No matter what your circumstances, you can still live life to the full. We don't know everybody's stories; what is their Everest is different from my Everest'.[3] Listening to Ian, how he has overcome his own barriers, and learning that the ethos of Olympianism is to inspire others to realise their potential, his words echo those of Paul, exchanging hindrance for running with perseverance. (By the way, he was 'absolutely rubbish at school sport', third place in a wheelbarrow race aged 8 the only hint at subsequent glories.) Hope forms the second angle of our triangle by embracing my unexpected medical journey as a fit and active runner, always looking to push myself further, yet stopped in my tracks and unable to run.

If you're not interested in medical details, just see this as an education into something I'm pretty sure you would never have heard of. Until I was diagnosed in 2014, I would have assumed a 'cavernoma' to be the name of an electronic piano keyboard, not a cluster of abnormal blood vessels on the brain or spinal cord. Approximately 100,000 people in the UK have a brain cavernoma without symptoms , but I found myself in a much smaller group (1 in 400,000) of those diagnosed with a *symptomatic* brain cavernoma.[4] I'm not interested in painting a picture for sympathy, but this is a crucial corner within our triangle if I am to describe what hope has come to mean for me.

Life has strange moments of irony, doesn't it? Thirty-three years ago, I was trusted with a lead role as the Scarecrow in my primary school's production of *The Wizard of Oz*. My thick hair has always felt like straw but they told me I was chosen because I could sing in tune. I can still remember fooling around the stage, straw coming from every possible pocket of my costume and of course, the required floppy hat. My solo was a song entitled 'If I Only Had a Brain'. Were my teachers telling me something in this amusing song about head-scratching, the occurrence of useful thoughts and conversing with nature? But life came full circle five years ago when I indeed required a healthy brain and needed fixing, because when cavernomas bleed, life has to stop. So here begins the medical story with a reflection I wrote upon returning home from hospital in 2014 . . .

Waking on Tuesday 20 May was a sensation I had never experienced before. My left arm had apparently fallen asleep making it impossible to button a shirt for work. No pain, no alarming symptoms, just part of me that felt like it needed carrying along with my rucksack into A&E that morning. Quickly seen by a nurse, I was soon crossing those lines reserved for poorly relatives, always for others – never for me. Lying on a hospital trolley at the peak of my cycling rush hour, injections and blood tests rapidly invading my fears of all things surgical.

As my wife was carrying out the school run (in the car) as normal before heading into the city for a law exam, the script of the day was being rewritten with a word I had never paid much attention to before – stroke. Disbelief and panic overwhelmed me as the heroes of our NHS talked me through the next stages of brain scans and the implications of the results – a bleed on my brain and an emergency transfer to King's College Hospital. A further implication was delaying the breaking of such news to my law-student wife, but I recalled her boundless forgiveness in our marriage so far and opted to lean upon that for now.

I don't know where that day went, but it was evening before the superheroes in green arrived ready to push the boundaries of time travel. Hurtling down the M20 lying in the back of an ambulance renewed my sense of fear, rather like being in a very loud contraption from the drawing board of Aardman Animation's Wallace and Gromit. The paramedic was superb beside me though produced no Wensleydale, assuring me that 'the pay kept the wrong sort of people out of this job' and that an uneven road surface that nearly saw us airborne was 'only Maidstone'. As we neared London, I kept hearing ambulances before the paramedic reminded me that *we* were the siren. A safe arrival at King's and onto the next job of the evening for my two guardian angels; light in the darkness, albeit flashing and blue.

Sleep in broken bursts and repeated interviews from hospital staff meant that I was pleased to hear the building site of a Camberwell dawn. Steel girders were lifted outside the window as I began my first lunar module manoeuvre – sitting up. Very soon I became aware of the team around me; patients with whom suffering forged a bond beyond words, where just a look seems to be enough empathy for now, and staff who were to show the utmost care and speak to me deeply. But on this day, I had little idea of the extent of my haemorrhage, or what would happen next. How often we live in an artificial world of guarantees, predictable routines and best-laid plans. Suddenly I could see the illusion for what it was, sat staring at my hospital stockings and non-slip red ankle socks straight from a Christmas ad for GAP, feeling slightly ridiculous, but as dress sense ebbed away, becoming more out of control and letting go.

Ever the recovering story-teller with a weakness for finding meaning before the lesson is fully completed, I found the shape of Christ's cross in the ceiling tiles above me. Lying on my back and looking up I became frustrated at my inability to find God in my pain. Tears flowed as I confessed to my wife, 'I just cannot find him.' That's the difference, I guess, between knowing and really *knowing*.

Waves of kindness were soon to break, a nurse who met any need with a smile and an older Irishman who silently swept the floor each morning. In fact, the names of caring staff were to become a reassuring theme throughout this experience as the journey to theatre for an angiogram was to forge another all-too brief friendship with a very encouraging nurse with two feisty children of her own at home. We spent waiting time discussing private health care, again leading me to the conclusion that the National Health service I was receiving was first rate, with qualities of encouragement in abundance.

A surgeon then introduced himself who had clearly worked harder than I did when at school. He explained the procedure about to take place before meeting me in a room that appeared straight out of sci-fi, with a giant plasma screen big enough to make a schoolboy drool. I had shared the likely odds of me passing out as Grace draped a cold compress of sympathy across my head, but to my surprise I was to push through like the great footballer Terry Butcher memorably once did for England against Sweden in a World Cup qualifier. Forget three lions on your chest, I had about three hairs after they prepared me for surgery.

Choosing not to watch the feature on the giant screen to which the surgeon was glued (as he appeared to be installing a Sky network in my leg), I opted to hum songs until I was asked by the team to keep very still. This was the moment where the optic cable neared the base of my brain, at which point I was treated to a 'firework' display as predicted; sparks of charges, I suppose, announcing themselves in bright orange glimpses, astonishing and on cue. Isn't the body just a complete miracle? After a painless few minutes my 'A star' graduate resorted to the old-fashioned method of applying pressure to the blood clot in front of him while I embarked upon another interview with a health professional. It transpired that neurologists have a hunger for learning, their careers a process of building knowledge upon knowledge.

The previous day I had been wheeled down by a cheerful porter for an MRI scan, another cause for prayer when faced with the claustrophobia of an Iron-Man face mask. Sickness truly finds a person out; the many times I pray in panic, treating it as a form of divine insurance. The reality of suffering sheds light upon our true reliance upon prayer, my many hopeful monologues exposing my mistreatment of what Jesus modelled as relationship with the Father. In Jesus, prayer was exampled as respiration, not superstition. My survival instinct was to liken the repeating electronic pulse to a Muse gig I'd attended a few months previously, occupying my imagination through tightly closed eyes before I replayed running the London Marathon which ticked all the boxes of endurance I was needing. I returned to base camp knowing I had faced a fear.

Back on the ward and starting a conversation with my new Irish friend, I discovered his national passion and pride in Brian O'Driscoll, the heroic Irish centre recently retired from international rugby. While my awareness of God was still murky, we had at least led each other to 'Bod', as O'Driscoll is known. One soon becomes accustomed to the rhythms of hospital wards and staff handovers, so evening passed and morning came. Another day of creative friendships – another day of hope.

It is significant to mention that I enjoyed two years of training in church leadership just a stone's throw from my hospital bed. To that end, my journey had a sense of 'coming home' to King's, as a steady stream of friends from college days appeared at my bedside over time, most of whom avoided the neatness of pastoral clichés but firmly playing the chaplaincy card to access the ward when they chose. Surely the lady at the desk would smell a rat at the conclave of Salvation Army ministers queuing up for conversation? Nonetheless, these encounters proved immensely fulfilling as I felt that my changed circumstances gave me permission to be direct and honest with each visitor. After all, we're all somewhat 'under the weather' regarding the fullness of life offered by Jesus, there being no underdog in any encounter but each party equipped to contribute equally of themselves. So, it became a time of cementing friendships, of agreeing on what is important in life, confessing the grey areas of faith and affirming each guest in turn.

This had become a time of hope, God revealing himself not through a coincidental sign that I was fortunate enough to spot, but through lives intersecting thanks to the traffic lights holding red. Each person was a reminder that light overcomes the dark[5] and as we share in each other's weakness we find permission to keep moving forwards in the mayhem of our rushing around, our i-lives where an Apple device a day keeps so much good away, I had been reminded that the dignity of life needs celebrating. Sharing without fear or judgement, we may bear the occasional signpost that calls others on to the next landmark. But even if we don't, feeling rather empty-handed with our Lucozade and bunch of grapes, our greatest words can simply be, 'I know, I've been there too.'

True friendship, like true discipleship, ought to be a humanising process. Some of us have never known it, embarrassed by the soft focus of sharing emotion. But if you ever dare to share your scars and stories, we play a part in each other's healing. Nouwen would refer to such as 'wounded healers',[6] and lots of them arrived, bringing hope, during those five days in King's.

That reflection was the first time I truly put pen to paper about suffering in my life, because it always seemed to be surprisingly accompanied by hope, like two sides of a coin – picking up one meant picking up the other. It was my debut reaction to the party line about a Christian fullness of life, which had started to worry me. A life without pain is a knee-jerk reaction to defending a good God, but when your leg won't move and knee won't jerk you look for something different, a new kind of hope.

As an example, for all its merits I get frustrated at the predictive text capability of my smartphone because every time I write 'haemorrhage' it wants to write 'heterosexual'. Now I know for a fact that I haven't written anything near this in electronic correspondence since I first played with an upside-down calculator in a dull maths class, probably around the time I sang as a scarecrow. Text-guessing opts for the common option, but sickness was the beginning of a blue line away from predictable, tame faith which avoids the unpredictable, leading me towards a wild hope which embraced it. Ken Costa so eloquently describes this hope as like a tiger, rather than the more usual expression of Christian hope as 'a pussycat, a good feeling'.[7]

I would love to roll credits and end with hope there, but that was only the start and I had more to learn. A further haemorrhage in the summer of 2015 led to the need to confront my fear of brain surgery that winter, a craniotomy, a word which still sounds industrial and clumsy to me. Could this be the end of the matter? Having geared myself up for this mentally, I will never forget coming round from the anaesthetic to be told by my consultant that after six hours and three attempted routes into my brain navigating eloquent areas, the operation was unsuccessful due to risk of left-sided paralysis in my arm and leg, so the cavernoma remained. Where do you go with such news? How do you move on? Symbolically, my wife suggested we go out and buy a new pair of trainers, some New Balance (I was lacking physical stability at the time too) which would be worn for my next race. Great idea, and I still wear them as a training shoe. Only a runner would understand the joy of new trainers but they smelt great in the box. Having lifted the lid off my head, my consultant also suggested the 'wait and see' path of treatment, allowing the cavernoma to behave in its own way, but in the meantime his words were 'now just go and get on with your life', which I did.

Getting on with life for me means running, so eleven months later I lined up for my first Royal Parks Half marathon, wearing New Balance trainers. It was an amazing run with a brain fully aware of sensory stimulation through a rural London – the smell of cut grass, the slush of autumn leaves beneath my feet as nature's falling jigsaw snuffed out the last rumours of summer picnics. My training over the summer had gone well and I PB'd in a time of 1 hour 43 minutes and 34 seconds (seconds are important when you tell your friends who are also runners). For me this race was a line in the sand; I needed to put down a marker for my health and make a statement to myself that life could be good again; the confidence to run, to be a husband, a father, to be employable.

At this point I want to mention the hope that lies in miraculous healing. Jesus performed many miracles in Scripture and I have always wanted my faith to honour the fact that his life ushered spiritual and physical restoration, God's '*kingdom*' activity was at hand. I personally experienced it when training for the 1998 marathon when I had overworked both my calf muscles and was in pain for weeks, wearing compression bandages but, inexperienced, not easing up on pounding the unforgiving concrete pavements of Ilford, Essex. It was at a healing session of the Alpha course in my church at the time that I prayed earnestly that God might heal my calves – and I choose to believe that he did. No more pain and I made the starting line months later. But compare that with a brain scan before my first surgery where I had again committed the problem to God for healing. My consultant walked towards me in the waiting area with the results to which I buoyantly asked, 'Has the cavernoma disappeared?' He smiled, 'I'm afraid not.' Healing can appear as a cruel lottery, a knife edge we walk, balancing our feet heal to toe, but let me assure you that it features within God's repertoire of hope because he evidently heals, as I have already said – *sometimes*.

Just over one year after the Royal Parks, a focal seizure[8] while driving the car confirmed my worst fears; the cavernoma was active again, haemorrhaging. Repeated seizures (a new symptom for me and one which I found exhausting and distressing) saw a very quick decision regarding a second craniotomy, because a blood clot can provide a safe entry route through the brain. Time is of the essence, so with my swollen brain slightly opened, the haemorrhage gave safe access for the surgeon. I never thought I would *choose* brain surgery, but this was actually what I wanted this time and in days the cavernoma was finally removed. You will have noticed that the haemorrhage meant my consultant could now perform successful surgery, victory from apparent defeat, a resurrection metaphor – see how hope shows itself again?

I confess that the pendulum of illness and recovery, improving my running then not being able to run at all, would have made me a wonderful case study for Elisabeth Kübler-Ross, the American-Swiss psychiatrist.[9] I experienced various stages of grief; the denial, anger and bargaining that come with traumatic change. However, I do not recall moving into accepting, because I was informed that, with physio and perseverance, I would run another marathon. But there was one afternoon where hopelessness came close to me; due to building work and scaffolding outside I hadn't seen daylight for days, a rhythm that running has also taught me to love. But my pace-setter friend Gordon dropped by, wicked with his sense of humour but always a wise man. It was towards Christmas 2017, so this arrival leads nicely towards my conclusion for this chapter with a reference to the Nativity story.

We know wise men brought three gifts to Jesus: gold – a gift for a King, frankincense – signifying Jesus' priestly role and a scent to encourage religious worship, and myrrh – a burial ointment signifying Jesus' significant death to come.[10] I'd received three visits; nurses repeatedly telling me that my heartbeat was very slow although I assured them that I wasn't yet dead (myrrh not needed), a cousin in a paisley-patterned shirt which set off such neural activity that I secretly saw stars during his entire visit (frankincense not really needed either), and finally Gordon with a gift that meant gold to me. I had never heard of the *Welcoming Prayer* of Mary Mrozowski of Brooklyn, New York,[11] but he suggested I try this contemplative tool and use the centring practice of neither reacting to stressful thoughts nor resisting them. It works in three stages: focusing on and sinking into the feeling, welcoming the feeling and ac-knowledging God's presence in the moment, and then letting go of the feeling by giving it to God. No point me lying there day after day saying to myself 'I can't stand needles' when I know that hospitals and needles are pretty much two ends of the same sharp instrument.

As I put this into practice, I began to gain courage, con-sciously committing my fears to God. It helped me to see that God is in all things, and that there are no parameters to his presence, not even pain. If God is not ever present, I cannot live with him, nor should anyone. My character finds it hard to sit still and we runners tend to be edgy, rarely idle. On an average day, before I have reached the bathroom mirror, my brain fires in many directions simultaneously, sometimes meaning that I take on too much and cannot focus or prioritise effectively. I'm recognising this as my true illness, perhaps why I found the *Welcoming Prayer* so hard to confront? But I am now attracted to slow; I use every step on every staircase, and after a lifetime of clamouring towards the influencers, I am increasingly drawn to 'the quiet ones', people who make less noise but radiate com-posure and consistency, qualities of God's prescription.

I'm not quite there yet with the *Welcoming Prayer*; I often forget to use it, but I know how much I need to do so, so I'll persevere because I've seen enough of hospitals to have begun a recalibration of fullness of life away from physical red her-rings. Hydration stations are vital in long-distance running and Gordon had offered me some water on an afternoon when I desperately sought the blue line. I had shared my fears and my friend, who has been a pace-setter all my adult life, had handed me hope.

8

Love

I see people; they look like trees walking around.[1]

I suggested in Chapter 1 that when we came to this third point of our triangle consisting of faith, hope and love, that love would be represented by running – an act I love. At that stage, I was excited by the prospect of devoting a whole chapter to this, but as it has grown closer, the task seems much harder; I may not convince you that running is loveable, you may have memories of strict PE teachers who made you run in the snow wearing baggy shorts and soaked socks, but when you begin to love something you don't always waste time worrying about how it is going to sound to others, such is love's consuming power. This chapter is about the difference running makes to me, not just physiologically but psychologically, the brain-body phenomenon which has helped me to love myself and others.

It's not just me who has found a love within sport, there are others too; leader friends, who used to confide their frustrations in me about people missing church and choosing to ride bikes or run races instead, are now also squeezing training into their weekly schedules and sharing my passion for that missing something; an itch that traditional gatherings within church buildings just cannot scratch. As you will have found, this book is partly about that very issue.

A wife was asked how her husband reconciled his Methodist convictions with the fact that most races are held early on Sunday mornings, replying, 'Tom used to be a Methodist. Now he's a runner.'[2] Running's salutary meaning found its way into James Fixx's *Complete Book of Running* with a chapter devoted to what happens to your mind, where he observes runners' language about its religious qualities or people becoming true converts. Fixx identifies running's insistent, hypnotic rhythms, which create a mental state in which runners feel remarkably at peace with the world and their significance within it.[3] Sounds like the work of Jesus to me. What if this is proof that God is in all things, the air we breathe, the people we meet, all we see from our miraculous bodies in which he dwells?

I have a unique friend ironically named John Smith, a man who has lit up rooms for as long as I can remember with a perennial sense of humour and glass half-full outlook. Jonny has been present most of my life but became a running convert after me, completing at least ten marathons by now and even one Ironman (as he insists on telling everyone). Jonny is one of life's pace-setters; he inspires me spiritually, relationally and since he ran a Sub 4 marathon has made me determined to keep chasing after his time, but he would testify that sport has sustained him, and it is likely that without it Jonny would not be his best self. Yes, he's a Christian, but he wouldn't choose a life without running.

One of my childhood memories is riding my BMX five minutes to my nan's house, clumsily scraping my knuckles along a narrow side alleyway to enter their back door and be served the most delicious carrots you could imagine. Bike discarded on the ground, back wheel still spinning, these carrots had a special quality. I have since learned that this was simply the taste of much salt in the cooking and serving, but you never forget your best childhood feasts, your first loves. I didn't need encouraging, but one of the fables banded around by post-war generations looking to enhance your peacetime health and wanting you to grow strong, was that carrots could 'help you to see in the dark'. I don't even know the science, but like most things you are told in childhood I believed in this supernatural power of carrots. Considering love, I know that our passions do empower us to see beyond the hard times; find something you love, stay in touch with people you love and you do indeed become able to see in the dark. Getting the difficult times in perspective, having somebody alongside you to cheer you on (in Jonny's case, somebody to laugh at me) is critical to surviving what life serves up.

You have probably gathered that I fell in love with running some time ago. Even in hospital, the hope of my next run was never far from my mind, probably because it represents my normal life rhythm and the familiarity of control. It was running that first enabled me to step off the treadmill of others' expectations and invest time in purely being alone. Murakami describes it like this: 'When I'm running I don't have to talk to anybody and don't have to listen to anybody. All I need to do is gaze at the scenery passing by. This is a part of my day I can't do without . . . I run in order to acquire a void.'[4] That void is a place I've come to know. There's nothing weird about it; in fact, it's become a meeting place for me and a springboard of my love for God and other people. I can see now how I had neglected it in my faith development, and how God has graciously come into it, perhaps knowing that I don't just love running, but want to love him. Sometimes, he makes me notice passers-by during my Sunday run, a lady with a sad face who cuts a lonely figure walking her dog; a silhouette that makes me pray over her day ahead (she will never know), and other runners whose faces I've come to recognise give a knowing grin as we pass in mutual respect. I often pray for friends with whom I experienced Bible college, knowing that if I'm running at dawn on Sundays, this is the day and time they are probably setting up for their church gatherings, switching on the heating, photocopying, wondering if anyone will show up; I remember the days.

I once perceived my missed routines as the fracturing of what God wanted to give me, but where Bible, pen and notebook were the symbols of my commitment to pray (and sometimes still are), today I am allowing my trainers and kit, left ready at the front door on a Saturday night, to be an equally powerful weapon. I often pray for my family and resolve to spend more time with my children when I'm out running, as if their absence or the miles I've created on foot have allowed my lens to widen and remember that they are crucial to the picture of my roles in life. During my seven years as a minister within The Salvation Army, I tried to hone such receptivity to God, but I didn't quite realise this default setting within me for distance running. It appears paradoxical, but I find better mental stillness through activity than sitting on my hands and extrinsically conforming like a cornered schoolboy waiting for 3 p.m. and home time.

This love relationship has been a complete surprise and I did not expect to become more reflective through running. When I run I feel free, it costs me nothing, I just go – I like to think of it as *freelaxation*. Running means that I breathe the air, some days I cannot see through sweat falling from my eyelids, others I feel the rain on my face, even laugh into the wind. Sometimes

I get to see the vivid palette of a secret sunrise in the dawn of a weekend, a brief gift for the early few. Listening to my body, experiencing the capacity of my lungs, the road beneath me, lost in thought and ticking away time, deliberately placing my feet for the right cadence, my arms for the right economy and speed, I remember I am a complex miracle of muscles and organs working in unity, oxygen pumping through, igniting my recovering brain as unforced decisions are made about family and work, occurring to me like free gifts. I escape in running and feel good, good enough for God and for those I have the pleasure to know. Freelaxation is the best of life.

As I describe this love, I can hardly believe where I was seven weeks ago. Hospital wards can be strange places where people wander and try to escape. I understand this; it can be exhaustingly tedious. When I was in the thick of neurosurgery recovery, all I could do was watch them; people out of context, patients adjusting to life. I too was clumsy, slow, picking up my left leg like a tree trunk and placing it where it needed to go next. Moves were calculated, manipulating items on my breakfast tray with the considered processes of a chess grandmaster; life less than its best, you could say.

But I never lost my sense of humour while people were watching. At one point, when a successful morning was to manoeuvre my Zimmer frame to the bathroom to brush my teeth, I caught sight of an older gentleman who gave me an empty smile, toothless, like one of those sinister dramatic icons. Seeing them on the side, I considered asking if he'd like me to take his teeth too, brushing both sets while I'm up? Then there was the nurse with a foreign accent frequently asking me, 'Are you Colin?' to which I just shook my head. I know the NHS is under pressure, but could this really be mistaken identity? I'd not exactly been bombing around the ward or swinging between the beds to confuse her, my full name was even written on the mini whiteboard above my bed, so we clarified that I was leaning on a buzzer alarm which made the staff believe I was *calling* – not Colin. The truth is that we all start to lose it a bit 'inside', and I was missing running.

Watching confused people reminded me of a blind man who was healed by Jesus in a place called Bethsaida.[5] Significantly, the touch of Jesus on his eyes does not seem to work the first time, as quoted at the start of this chapter. He sees general shapes, what appears to be 'trees walking around', detecting movement but not with clarity. Not experiencing clear sight the first time, Jesus touches his eyes a second time before the miracle of full vision comes to him.

I hold my hands up in saying I have not always seen people in the way God sees them, my love hardly living up to that modelled by Jesus, and I need the second touch. More dangerously still, I have snacked upon the crumbs of Christianity at the expense of the feast of fullness of life, doing token good things to impact people's lives as opposed to truly empathising with their pain, happy to pull them off the battlefield in heroic mission but inconvenienced if I have to wait alongside them in the trenches, just in case they demand too much. I'm not the most empathic of people; if only my love was patient, kind, without envy and kept no 'record of wrongs',[6] as I'm sure my wife and children will echo.

It is in this sense that running has got me on God's operating table. I've chosen to use running as an expression of love in this chapter, but it needs to be far more than the celebration of a hobby I hold dear. As with the physical manifestations of God associated with churches in Toronto, Canada, during the

1990s called the 'Toronto Blessing', it wasn't so important that God's Spirit made people fall over backwards, but more important was *who they were when they got up*. What had this intimate 'blessing' encounter done within them? And I apply the same test to the hours I invest running around in life.

I know that running deals with me biologically and spiritually, it unravels the knots in my personality and my self-set religious expectations. I have begun many runs with tight shoulders, burdened by thoughts and pressures, only to feel them lifted through the act of moving and breathing deeply. The production of endorphins, the brain's 'feel-good' chemicals, sets to work. It is no surprise therefore that one of my favourite magazines, *Runner's World*, always features people's stories of hope and recovery from health or mental traumas because endorphins reduce our perception of pain and anxiety which is often associated with depression.

To runners, recording their gallant efforts utilises apps like Strava, but for me I've always been a striver. So, what is there not to love about such a state of happiness, which for a religionist like me has been a welcome arrival at my door. I wish that was describing Colin, but it sounds very much like me.

This was certainly true as a young adult working as a children's cabin counsellor in Calabasas, California for the summer of 1996 – a long, hot summer with snakes and tarantulas always a stone's throw away – 'working for God' yet crippled by self-consciousness as we lined up on our campsite for the daily rituals. Respecting the American culture at the time in which I was working, I joined in with the flag-raising and pledging allegiance. Before a dozen lines of tough American teenagers, one of the tanned home team of staff set eyes on me, the pale British red-head, and blurted out, 'Now, that is a white boy!'

Replay that phrase over in your mind enough times and you establish a neural pathway that makes you never want to put on a pair of shorts again, but running has put all that behind me.

Despite shop windows wanting you to believe otherwise, running is not essentially about image, and this is part of its beauty for me. It remains accessible because it is a personal journey, offering everyone the escape of being present in the moment, mindful, too focused on the next step to worry about being judged on appearances. When you have made time to get out on a straight road of an evening after a long day at work, when you have shared the anticipation at the start on a race day or when you are on track for your best-ever 5k and your heart feels like it could burst out of your chest, you really don't care about how white your factor 50 total-block legs are. A life without judgement from others is surely a fuller life.

Not being judged then replicates; after all the mistakes I've made and relationships that have become clogged and hard to unravel, running puts me in a solitary place where I can look to God again and recover some sight, realising the hurts I've caused but remembering that the blue line of a 'running God' does not keep score. So, I diary-in my running. The benefits that my family have commented upon mean that it's an appointment like any other, so I'm deliberate about it. (To put it another way, they know when I haven't run!) My normal routine is to prepare all my kit the night before with a check on the weather (always dress as if it is 10 degrees warmer because you will feel that way after 5 minutes' running), make sure my iPod and Garmin are charged, then set the alarm. Of course, when it is 6:30 a.m. and the rain is hammering down outside, you question your rationale, but once you are found by the Global Positioning System on your wrist and the body is warm, there lies the potential for finding another level of human existence.

By 7 a.m., come rain or shine, I lace up my trainers, excited by the inspiration I'm about to receive through the wisdom of teaching from familiar preachers Robinson, Zacharias or Wells, before my stride is further energised by Chaka Khan or Coldplay. It's like a table for one and I wish everyone could feel revival like it.

Some mornings my inspirational playlist has synced perfectly with a glimpse of nature, such as a display of the changing colour of a leaf (and, with a quick check around me – I have even high-fived the hanging branch of a tree!) and I am the happiest person on the planet. I don't properly understand why running and music make me want to cry at my age, and I'm giving up needing to know. Like dissecting a butterfly, I am prepared to just receive the pleasure of the music. British athlete Sir Roger Bannister, first man to run the Sub 4-minute mile in 1954, acknowledged the pleasurable impact of running upon the nervous system by comparing it to the stimulation of listening to Handel's *Messiah*.[7] I was thrilled when I discovered Bannister's marriage of running and music, especially because he worked as one of those professionals I have begun to see more of – a neurologist. I can only conclude that running facilitates a type of mindfulness in me, both of God and of those I live and work amongst, so I run towards love.

Finally, a word about my love for church, part of me which keeps cropping up in this book; not a building, not an event, but a community of people. Alan Jamieson, author of *Chrysalis*, received a letter from a reader who so desperately wanted to change his church's fortunes. I come across so many people similarly bruised. It contained words of deep emotion, exhaustion, someone for whom transforming a Christian church which haemorrhaged people had become a consuming passion. In defeat, he wrote to Jamieson, expressing his efforts to pull down the establishment with all the tools a builder might use for demolition, before being left at the foot of its untouched walls with only his tears, bruised fists and cries for it to change.[8] I empathise with this reader, and I am still a part of my own local church so that I can journey 'with' others as a discipline of love that I believe is necessary for me. However, I am also mindful that our church leaders are an easy target; they put their heads above the pulpit, their words stimulate our own conclusions and they are brave in sharing their hopes and dreams – what they love. Sometimes I moan about them, but running soon deals with that.

However, I will never forget the moment I returned from a long early Sunday morning run about six years ago, with soaked trainers from the dew on the grass, having listened to an inspirational sermon by Haddon Robinson before singing along to some incredible dance anthems on my way home. His work had pointed out the bookends of the race we are all on, this human race, clarifying that Jesus had not intended to make people who are bad, good, or people who are good, better, but for the spiritually dead to be brought to life. I don't follow Jesus to be a better person, I don't go to church because I'm secretly bad and want to be ahead of the next person in the queue at heaven's check-in; I just want to live more fully and see things more clearly, through eyes touched by Christ. My face beaming, sweat dripping, white-legged, feeling fully alive and with the clearest of vision, I had been on another running journey. Trapped inside my own thoughts initially, then abandoning them through exhaustion, before God started to break in and give me vision, helping me to see all that was good about life and his world.

My wife was slowly waking and I simply said, 'I think I have already been to church today.'

9

The Spirit of Christmas Past

He has brought down rulers from their thrones but has lifted up the humble. He has filled the hungry with good things but has sent the rich away empty.[1]

Charles Dickens's *A Christmas Carol* is a powerful story of three spirits visiting Ebenezer Scrooge.[2] The first of these, the Spirit of Christmas Past was famously used to reveal one man's downwards spiral into selfish living and stir within him the necessity to change his ways. It is a classic transformation story where the shaping of Scrooge's character descends before it can ascend. Flying over London, Scrooge is confronted with visions of his childhood, schooldays, young adulthood, the compassion of his first boss, Mr Fezziwig and his lost love, Belle. Scrooge can finally bear no more, and makes his best attempt to get rid of this spirit of Christmas Past, before trying to get back to sleep.

We have already done many of these things in this book; revisited schooldays, recounted turbulent times of health with flying visits to London, stumbled into compassionate people and waded through the experience of the lost love of church leadership. I hope that I am conveying that all transformation stories are as dim as Scrooge's candle flame in the light of the death and resurrection of Christ, itself the ultimate transformation story. So, for this chapter, I want to speak less about running and hold the fresh light of the Holy Ghost up against Christmas. What does God's Spirit reveal through my Christmases past?

Looking outside my window across the park on Christmas morning, running continues. Hundreds of joggers gather in Santa hats and fancy dress in the early light, forming a dazzling snake of red and green around the Parkrun's frosty paths. My family and I vow to join them next year but this December 2018 is the anniversary of one year since surgery and marks twelve months without seizures. Medically I am healed, and I feel grateful because winter has become a time when I have seen too much of hospitals. It is also a relief to my family who have been a terrific support and source of strength over the three winters when ambulance doors seem to have opened as often as those on my children's Advent calendars. I cannot stress their resilience enough, when King's College Hospital felt like a second home.

Christmases past have a new significance for me and have become a time when I have written much, so I want to draw these reflections together in true Dickens fashion using my own three challenges; the reality of Christmas, growing out of Christmas and Christmas as a time to wonder at the mystery of God.

Since my days of conscious faith began, the trigger for writing was the contrast between reality and presumed yuletide bliss which drew something out of me; confusion, frustration, sometimes anger. Equally, Christmas has the potential for peace, hope and joy. In childhood, it brought the conflict of expectation tainted by fear; going to bed to spend the next eight hours sweating like Scrooge, in the knowledge that a benevolent stranger who knew me by name would enter my room under the cover of night as I hid under the cover of bedsheets.

How did his knowledge span the globe and how did he know me? I think he symbolised much of what I hoped God would be like if I could ever meet him.

Outside of God, I do not do Christmas terribly well; I can live without the bloated self-indulgence and the consumerism masquerading as generosity, knowing full well that openness to others and consciousness of those without a home or meal are qualities that should know no season. In my initial years of faith, the mixed message of Santa sprinkled with a dusting of Christ was a slipper hard to fit. Surely the church had a mandate to respond clearly to this pantomime of ideas? I have since made my peace with seasonal trappings to the delight of my family, who saw me as their very own Mr Scrooge. Ironically, my children have grown up to absolutely love Christmas and I find myself outnumbered and overpowered to get into the spirit (whatever that is?) as I open the dusty, badly sealed boxes in the loft.

So, let's unwrap the first parcel, the Reality of Christmases past. Two thousand years ago, Jesus was born into a politically charged world, where an oppressive government did little to cater for the needs of displaced people.

In those days Caesar Augustus issued a decree that a census should be taken of the entire Roman world. (This was the first census that took place while Quirinius was governor of Syria.) And everyone went to their own town to register. So Joseph also went up from the town of Nazareth in Galilee to Judea, to Bethlehem the town of David, because he belonged to the house and line of David.[3]

David's town was not set for Joseph's welcome home party. The census stretched it physically, but I conclude that emotionally they could not easily be taken in, so he remained prodigal thanks to the gossip-mongering surrounding his misunderstood pledge to heavily pregnant Mary. There could not be a more biased reception or more chaotic scene; you and I have been there when we crave time to explain – minds working faster than reasoning; Joseph's worries of the night fearing the light of dawn. Our brains enter overdrive in the dark.

In December 2017, my brain cavernoma once again haemorrhaged after what had felt like a wonderful sabbatical. This caused whispers in the neighbourhood. Our front door became suspiciously like the arrivals' foyer of a Methodist convention, the body of Christ faithfully baking Word into flesh. In the heat of the moment the church really cares, of course, and the Pyrex party occurs because my wife and I have suddenly made the unplanned journey back to our own 'David's town', the home of previous medical treatment. Another Mary and Joseph; confused, emotionally jolted, I'm vaguely aware of a guiding star siren above while she navigates the donkey of London's rail network.

The New Zealand ambulance crew foretell the busyness of the capital while in my daze I am sure we could not have reached Wellington, even at 90 miles an hour. In true irony, our star rests above King's, workplace of my learned consultant and the hospital located opposite The Salvation Army's William Booth College where I trained in theology from 2001–03. It was here that my 'Word made flesh' neurons were first ignited, seeking truth, building friendships, dreaming dreams, like Joseph himself. A rolled-up scroll from a commissioning ceremony is increasingly a distant memory of birth into church leadership, but I am sure that Bethlehem had its mix of memories for Joseph too. Yet tonight, I return to this birthplace; Camberwell feels like David's town to me.

Bethlehem is heaving, it is third world despite 2,000 years of supposed progress. Bodies cramp corridors, makeshift first-aid tucks into quieter corners, birth dates are requested upon arrival because a system dictates. We sit opposite three policemen, stood on guard outside a secure room housing a sedated mental health patient. I gaze up at them wondering what the Roman guard makes of its government's own empire? And do they ask, like me, where God is in this mayhem?

Eventually light does come, as the freezing morning yawns and we continue our dawn waiting. Of course, we're not in labour, but nine hours of random blood tests in A&E are enough to convince me that critical veins of compassion have virtually collapsed in this society. Judaea's current issues of isolation, the threat to the dignity of the elderly, immigration and anxiety condense as I offer the diabetic next to me some water and the lady opposite breathes oxygen through a canister large enough to send her into orbit with the heavenly host.

In this modern breathless Bethlehem, I think of a lyric from Phillip Brook's[4] Victorian 'O Little Town of Bethlehem'; which 'mortals sleep, [while] the angels keep their watch of wondering love' tonight? Or who is going to get so much as a stable, as hospital bed managers do their best within this census carnage? Looking for God, I choose to notice the small things – the cracks of light in the unkept wood, the unswerving loyalty of Rome regardless of the hour, the potential meeting with wise men who may explain our journey later, the bed manager in neuro-admissions who smiles and gently talks to us, but thinks that finding a bed is highly unlikely until a miracle of sorts occurs – there is room in this inn.

So, we are admitted to events beyond our control as this
night gains momentum. It's easier to surf on my phone than
to pray, but I'm angered by the Christmas lie uploading to social media, decorations being hung by overheated families in
pixelated sweaters. Wake up, church! Those doorstep casseroles
say more than a church that has folded its woolly arms through
too many years of making flesh into word again. Because I see
that God is at work *here*; he's in the muck of stable and unsta-
ble, staff spinning plates, serving humankind, proving that in
the darkest of times compassion shines brightest. This is hu-
mans trying to remain so.

We are ushered into a quiet room with two comfortable
chairs and drips of blood across the floor. In the accompanying
paradigm shift, my wife and I are both grateful. I'm no longer
lying uncontrollably on the floor with my rucksack for a pil-
low being watched by a stone-faced centurion with stethoscope
who just stands, not even asking my name. I could not resent
him in my fear of seizure – he's afraid of his Caesar's targets
too. But as our hours of waiting end in these NHS wipe-clean
institutional chairs, other travellers continue to arrive in this BC
A&E. All come, rich and poor, kings and shepherds; London's
pinstriped commuters with calloused device fingertips slump
in surrender beside the sweaty site workers in hi-vis who have
known a very different day's work. This night was scheduled
for none, reality cares nothing for our diaries. We, Mary and
Joseph, are in a building that hosts both life and death, beginnings and endings; weeping happens here, humanity awakens.
It's tragic that we don't treasure rebirth more often.

At this point we can finally rest; rest without knowing the
days ahead, without knowing the necessary surgery or implications at the opening of this inconvenient Advent door. We can

rest knowing that God *has been with us in reality*, even though it did not hinge on us being treated to part of some divine string of preprogrammed plan of events tonight. Reality has kicked this idea to smithereens but God has been *within* our experience because it was indeed his own experience, and there can now be nothing outside the reach of Immanuel – 'God with us'[5] – even in this Bethlehem madness. Exhausted, I thank God for this very real Neuro-Nativity.

I would now like to talk about growing up as the second feature on my list of Christmases past. My first experience of being in control of my own music was a cassette featuring the 1980 song 'Super Trouper' by Swedish pop group Abba. It was harmonically rich, deeply formative and got under my 6-year-old skin in a way that injected some sort of goodness or optimism that I couldn't explain by a life lived in single digits; perhaps I was being Bjorn again? To gain further control, I needed a cassette recorder, so I drew up my list for Santa and included a recorder.

On Christmas morning with family gathered round, I unwrapped a long green plastic tube with Hohner printed on it in gold, which held a plastic pipe that produced different notes when I blew air through it and moved my fingers; I had got my recorder, exactly what I had requested. I was inwardly devastated, Abba cassette in one hand and recorder in the other. Santa had let me down. In later Christmases or birthdays, we rectified the problem and I remember finally receiving the most awesome cassette recorder, double cassette actually, by which point I'd moved from Abba onto Paul Hardcastle's '19'. My second gift from the ghost of Christmas Past is that we don't always get what we ask for.

Figures suggest that as much as 37 per cent of us receive an unwanted Christmas gift, spending £2.4 billion pounds in the process,[6] including uneaten food. One solution could be to supply loved ones with an early December shopping list, but others will always prefer the element of surprise. We are all somewhere on this spectrum, and at the time of Christ's birth there were similar shopping lists for God; what he would do, how he would reveal himself definitively as liberator, conqueror, the new King. There still exists such a God-list today as we crowbar the Nativity story into a hole which ticks every box of sentimentality and crowd-pleasing we can muster. But when we look closer at this text we begin to find that nobody, then and now, actually gets what they ask for.

Surrounding the incarnation is a series of experiences that fly against the wind of human expectation; God placed into the feeding trough of cattle, God who becomes human through a disgraced pregnant teenager despised by her community, God who risks rejection by Joseph as he causes him to probably mistrust his promised bride. This is not a narrative that lends itself to a warm reception; it is too shocking, too risky and too turbulent to be easily received. And I thank God for that and this is why – I have outgrown the Nativity story. It has been too clean and politically correct, making minimal impact upon the development of my faith. For it to play a credible part in my life, it must be a signpost to a God who's involved in the real world instead of some ethereal Bethlehem night where tranquillity reigns. This is all about growing up. To those burned by faith it must act as a reminder that God engages with the world in its most harsh realities, but I'm asking the question on the busiest night of the church's year, are we truly helping anyone if we don't clear away the tinsel and convey God's heart as he reaches out 'to those on whom his favour rests'?[7]

Our growing up comes down to our understanding of this word 'favour'. The angels announced that 'peace' would come to those subjected to God's favour and we read that those directly involved in the story are 'favoured' in the sense of being used by God to bring about events, chosen, set apart. But 'those' implies everyone, so what might we need to unwrap in order to receive what is needed instead of getting what we have childishly asked for? I believe it is this: God's favour is immensely richer than a quick fix to a panicked prayer when the petrol gauge on my car runs low; God as a baby in a manger signals his experience of frailty and vulnerability to match my own, crying in need, from cradle to cross. His favour is that he aligns himself with our experience of limited humanity, then works with that; the despised virgin, Mary, favoured in that God reveals himself to the most vulnerable girl who will put her trust in him; the confused Joseph, partially out of the loop, favoured in that God allows him to see who he cares about the most, testing his commitment to Mary and laying down his reputation in the name of faith. I can see myself in all of them; this is a story I need to hear.

This is a dramatic story and one of challenge. God's favour creates momentum when it rests upon people and shows that he then walks with them; peace through the turbulence. Surely this is much better Christmas news to deliver than just a baby, more relevant to all? Our default is to waste this season by opting for the easy experience of a magic God who 'does us all a favour' now and then, a Santa who always visits leaving the correct gift, but by looking more deeply at this text as an adult I have discovered a maturing significance.

No character illustrates this better than Mary. I began to appreciate Mary whilst standing at the base of two escalators in a clothes shop, waiting for my wife who was battling in a cubicle where the floor was probably strewn with plastic hangers. December in a women's clothes shop is every man's nightmare –

even Bear Grylls might struggle. I was gifted a few moments of stillness as the Paul McCartney shop soundtrack again told me that he was having a great Christmas, annoyingly. I had a choice, to escalate upwards or wait for whoever was to descend, and it was one of those awkward moments where, as devoted husband, I found myself loitering, texting anyone, like a teenager awkward in my own body with arms that feel 10ft long and really unsure how to stand. Even though I must have looked rather odd on CCTV I decided to stay put, interested in the opposite movements of the two escalators. They had got me thinking about traditional 'Last Judgement' paintings of the Renaissance period and how much of life the average fearful Italian spent considering whether their final journey would be up or down.

Heaven and hell are there in the biblical Christmas, should the Spirit lead you to find them. As with the story curve of Mr Scrooge, there are descents and ascensions. Upwards, shepherds are treated to sights of heaven's opera on tour above local hills, kings gazing and star-chasing, but conversely, the visit of the angel to Mary is a downward movement, God's realm descending to us, as ultimately occurred in Christ. This moment does not automatically lead to Mary rising to the heights of heaven but instead, as we have seen in our second strand, results in shameful, embarrassed downwards gaze; the consequent pregnant pause of those who knew her best. Less talked about is the dilemma she faced from her obedience to the angel's news. A paradoxical moment; Mary, gifted by the Holy Spirit to bear God's revealed son as heaven comes down is also Mary the teenage virgin looking her community in the eye and knowing the hell of disgrace. Mary, who had to confront the suspicion of adultery before Joseph, precisely because she was loyal and true to him, honouring God throughout her young betrothed life. Open to misunderstanding, this moment of favour from above appears to hold only a downwards future for the chosen: 'Do not be afraid, Mary, you have found favour with God.'[8]

Unfathomable plans remind us that God's ways are rarely our ways, nor is the Bible composed as a scam to convince or control its audience. It's a shame that it has taken such a beating, but we've probably invited it upon ourselves. This encounter teaches me that God's favour and our consequent obedience is by no means an easy ride upwards, but may take us further than we have ever been in risking identity and the judgement of those we love the most, an apparent ride downwards. Its authenticity lies in its unattractiveness, echoing my experience of fullness of life being nothing like a fast-pass to an improved circumstance. Mary knew her God humbly, taking hold of the freedom available in standing tall beneath his favour so, thereafter, man's was not half as important. She found poise in the presence of God's messenger, peace within the war of others' judgement and a place within God's purpose for humanity. If you are like me, such themes are not easy to stomach; downwards is painful when upwards is so much easier, but perhaps if we came to terms with this topsy-turvy favour then more of us would be ready to receive it. December advertising will always sell you personal upwards mobility; cook this and they will think that, buy this and they will say that; but the gaping hole in the seduction of your best Christmas ever is that God's favour comes to those who resolve themselves to the downwards consequences of it. Growing out of Christmas, when the simple tale ceases to satisfy, makes me thank God that we don't always get what we ask for.

Our third approach to Christmas Past is when the Spirit again sets to work and the season becomes a helpful time to pause in order to enter into wonder. Ten days before Christmas in 2015 I was forcibly paused, recuperating at home following an unsuccessful craniotomy, listening to my body and experiencing the odd sensation of post-surgery numbness down my left side that would arrive then soon disappear. It was unusual and made me momentarily panic, like having pins and needles while being inflated full of air. Each onset made me ask the hot-thought of: 'Will the leg return to normal? When will I be able to walk properly or write with a pen?' Slouched upon the lounge sofa, I felt like the England football team under Italian manager Fabio Capello, also known for having little to offer down the left-hand side.

I'm no Michelangelo's *David*, but these days, it's only my lopsided torso that gives the game away of previous strokes where my core has not symmetrically returned nor my left bicep returned to its original strength. However, this does not mean I run in circles, but have to work slightly harder to balance my form. Back then, anchored in my lopsided weakness, I was completely engrossed by the televised live launch from Baikonur Cosmodrome (southern Kazakhstan) of three wise men aboard the Soyuz rocket on its way to the International Space Station. Astronauts Tim Peake, Yuri Malenchenko and Tim Kopra had trained for years; knowledgeable in multiple languages, accomplished scientists, not to mention brave beyond belief. My family laugh at me because Tim Peake and I both have red hair and enjoy running (he was filmed running a virtual London Marathon on marathon day during his six months orbiting the earth) but I can assure you that this is where the similarities end because I shudder in the queue for the fairground teacups. Captivated by the events I was watching as that rocket left earth, my brain was firing perfectly whilst my leg lagged behind.

It seems that wise men know how to enjoy themselves, even while on serious business. As Major Tim was catapulted into space, becoming the first publicly funded British astronaut (funded by the European Space Agency) he could even afford a punched fist and several waves at the camera from his tiny capsule as it escaped the earth's atmosphere. I've seen a Soyuz capsule and, believe me, they are a baked bean tin of a spacecraft. Several hours later, they manually docked with the space station, wriggling through the open hatch to be greeted within their new home for the next six months. As I watched, I began to appreciate the knowledge these men possess; endless buttons and flashing switches line metal-panelled walls, where one error separates them from the hostile environment of outer space. Still Major Tim grinned constantly, exhausted from the journey but bursting with delight at his first 'great day at the office'.[9] Seeing such vulnerability superseded by joy, I connected emotionally with these three wise men miles above the earth and vowed to look out for the moving star that would be the ISS wherever possible during the coming winter nights, the sun reflecting against its solar panels as it sped across our dawn and dusk skies.

The dual purpose of their journey involving technical skills of achieving the correct orbit and speed, was to explore and to share. Tim Peake's experiments were to enthuse a new generation of schoolchildren in how the human body reacts to living in space. His dramatic pilgrimage was just the beginning; from now on his human life will be responding to the elements from its changed view of the world.

The crew of the Soyuz had been lifted up but remained humble in their hunger to learn, echoes of Mary's visit and three-month stay with her cousin Elizabeth in the biblical account, words which opened this chapter. I took their mission as a timely reminder of the wise men chasing down a star, finally arriving at a place saturated in unknowns, but ready to seek, to learn and to share what being human really means. I will never know the impact of a window seat from space upon the earth, but from my window seat on the sofa I was filled with wonder, my third lesson from a Christmas past.

These three Christmas insights, or indeed three gifts, have given me the opportunity to replace old expectations with a dose of reality, an opportunity to grow up and time to pause in wonder. I'm well enough to report that the Tempro is increasingly intriguing and continues to attract me; this line I keep talking about – yes, it means following an unusual star, but God has always dealt in uncertainties. God has used Christmases past to gift me these three insights of reality, growing up and wonder. I want to conclude this chapter by drawing these strands together and using them as a launchpad, like a short gulp of Lucozade to a runner, before exploring the interplay of faith, hope and love more widely. So here is the energising breathing space; how shall you and I deliberately make a better job of next Christmas? How shall we turn a 'no' into a 'yes'?

I was once queueing up for a carol service outside Canterbury Cathedral, an annual pilgrimage for my family because it serves up a balancing dose of wonder for my children. Standing outside the vast home of the worldwide Anglican Church, building work was underway. As with most of our cathedrals and like a decent faith, it seems that they are forever under construction and needing renewal.

A car squeezed its way through a narrow makeshift road, hitting bollards either side where there was quite obviously little room. I bent down to peer inside, my face half-bemused and half-annoyed at the driver's window, then laughed at God's reminder to me to keep prising open the door of my life, saying 'yes' and welcoming him in. I had made eye-contact with the Archbishop of Canterbury.

The Nativity plays forget to tell us that when God came amongst us he wanted to work with us; we are to yield, to welcome him in the form he chooses, whoever our neighbour happens to be; from speaking parts to stage hands, just as Mary was open to Gabriel. Faith and hospitality are needed, enough for the creativity of God to accomplish his will through us. It takes just one voice, one 'yes'. When he asks, we have a choice, although I fully empathise with the obsession over reputation that causes panic in the Herods amongst us. But from now on, I hope I don't miss God when he arrives; life feels too short. I want to live prepared; a life on the lookout, a welcoming life instead of a judgemental one, where people are joined together instead of isolated; qualities which I now associate with a runner's life. If I see Christ's face staring back at me, all the better. I'll be expecting him.

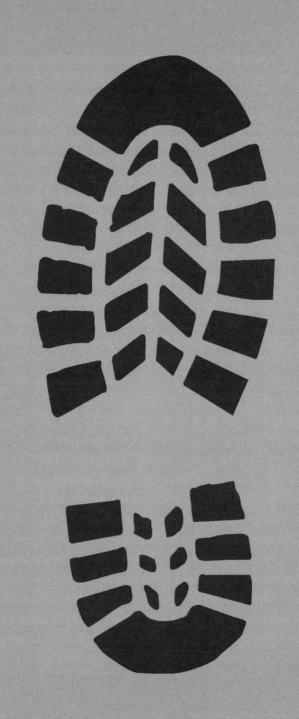

10

When Faith and Hope Speak to Each Other

I want to know Christ – yes, to know the power of his resurrection and participation in his sufferings, becoming like him in his death, and so, somehow, attaining to the resurrection from the dead.[1]

Playmobil has always been a favourite in our house. We have a Nativity set that comes out each Advent, taking centre stage in our lounge for around ten years. Of all the intricate pieces which are added daily as the season progresses, the one which catches my eye (because I don't really understand the physics) is the cooking pot which hangs from a tripod of plastic sticks. On their own the sticks cannot stand up, neither can two of them, but when the three intersect at just the right angle they move from delicacy to strength. I've even taken this piece apart and rebuilt it just to understand why it works so well. (Yes, I do need to get out more!) This book commenced by setting out the three lines of faith, hope and love, as the triangle in which I wished to explore the relationship between running and believing. Having established their individual significance to me personally, I now want to explore the mutual impact of the parts upon each other and their consequent strengthening, commencing with the remoulding of my faith through a time of illness; when faith and hope met.

Being rather competitive, I have always been suspicious of the phrase 'It's not the winning, it's the taking part that counts', but as a school teacher who believes in inclusivity, I appreciate its merit. Creeping into home decoration shops packed with distressed-style hanging signs, I often come across similarly engraved driftwood telling me that destinations are far less important than journeys. I pause, unsure of how this stacks up against so much fear of hell and judgement in my formative Christian years, consoling myself with the biblical precedent of the wise men who did not know the end of their star-chasing tour but moved obediently into the twists and turns of the darkness, navigating the threats of a power-crazed King Herod. But what if, like me, you are quietly someone who prefers to know a happy ending before you set off? Motivational posters carrying isolated Christian texts often want me to hear such neat messages: 'I press on towards the goal to win the prize for which God has called me heavenwards in Christ Jesus.'[2] No doubt this is destination language, winning language, there is a prize at the end.

Focus upon happy endings resonates with me because I sometimes have to cycle over a fairly narrow bridge to get to our local hospital, which crosses the M20 motorway in Kent. If I do not look straight ahead to the other end of the bridge, I notice the traffic flying past below, finding that my legs go wobbly and I cycle diagonally. Bizarrely, I do exactly what I don't want to do, so I can see the wisdom in eyeing up the end of the bridge. Even so, I'm still in two minds about the trajectory of God's blue line. Is it about eyeing up heaven's finishing line and winning (having answers to everything), or is it more about taking part (living with questions instead)? I do know, however, that I don't want an escapist, exit theology to this world of suffering, but at the same time I know that developing resilience is not always much fun. This leaves me looking for a real faith in the real world, so in this chapter winning and taking part collide. What do fullness of life and illness have to say to each other?

I'm fortunate to be a runner because I've physically experienced a fullness of life through sport. I've had bucketloads of inspiration through watching running races or being a participant, all of which speak to me as glimpses of heaven. I once watched a friend in his first marathon coming through Greenwich and he waved as I shouted from the crowd. The thousands of bodies, the spectrum of running vests, a tribe of momentum so countercultural to a stranger-averse London any other day of the year, made me emotional as I watched him make progress after all the hard months of training and life-impacting preparation. I believe that love reigns recklessly in heaven, and watching marathons whispers to me that East and West sit down together in the diverse kingdom of God.

Such moments fuel my desire to run, to be part of it, swept up in the tide. Running with others just creates an effervescent joy within me, a life-full sensation, and this happened in my 2012 London Marathon. I was running in support of Care for the Family, a charity whose work rang true with my own as a primary school teacher and parent[3] and gave me that extra lift on some of the harder training nights. It happened in the darkness of the Blackfriars Underpass just before we emerged into the daylight and crowds along the Thames Embankment. The underpass is a few miles from the finish but provides minutes of silence where some runners stop with cramp, some hit the wall while others urinate up it. Etiquette has pretty much disappeared by this point because the mind plays havoc.

I was running within a pack of around a hundred people, the rhythm of our trainers bouncing off the walls, audible because no one dared speak, or had the energy to. But I did not feel alone, I felt joy and had to find an outlet for it. I was thinking about God, chewing over my years of faith and striving, the twists and turns of my life – the darkest moments, while feeling that every person around me carried their baggage too, and my instinct was to unite them. 'You can't shout out loud! You don't know anyone! What if they don't respond? You will look a fool' – the monologue played over in my head several times until suddenly I burst out with, 'Oggy Oggy Oggy!' I could not believe it, I'd never put myself on the line in this way before, what on earth was I doing? Yet within seconds, an army replied, 'Oy oy oy!' This call and response bouncing off the walls of that underpass was a sound I will never forget; the hairs on the back of my neck stand on end as I write. It was a moment of unity, shoulder to shoulder, of shared suffering and endeavour, and I knew we were going to make it home, just like I know I will with God one day. A glimpse of fullness of life for me.

As well as glimpses of joy, I find it equally helpful to discover that suffering recalibrates inflated ideas around fullness of life. Feel-good messages can threaten maturity of faith and we must be cautious of the motivational slogans across Christian bookshops or conferences that 'God has amazing things for us to do'. I am living proof that the bubble can burst, having broken a signed covenant within The Salvation Army to 'love and serve him supremely all my days'.[4] Did I let God down when I decided that I couldn't continue doing such amazing things any longer and walked away from my calling? Believe me, as I relocated my young family towards the Kent coast in 2010, parallels of Jonah headed for Tarshish by sea were not lost on me.[5] The truth is that I knew church planting had taken its toll when I walked into a school staffroom where I had been leading an assembly and simply wanted to hang around, needing company. The isolation of leading a rural church had made me reflective to an unhealthy degree and I wanted to belong to others, or would probably lose my mind.

There have been some emotional runs since then and through distance running, God has quietly whispered that I still serve him supremely. A sudden or traumatic change in circumstances is proof that heroic 'winning' Christianity is a smokescreen and that existing patiently through the ordinariness of 'taking part' remains the most valuable development for an egocentric God-chaser like me. Because taking part is fellowship with God.

Fellowship with God can therefore be both our future and our present experience, bearing Jesus' own example – to do the Father's will, at work, in our homes and in our communities. Then, when we are woken from surgery to disappointing news, fullness of life actually becomes that very fellowship which walks towards such news, as we saw in the *Welcoming Prayer*. Christ wants our partnership; it is the biggest compliment or act of worship we can give. His life was not merely successful as a barcode into heaven; he was too involved in people's lives in the present and suffered himself with no 'get out' other than hoping in God. This confrontation with the darkness of despair by the 'luminous Nazarene'[6] is for us to follow – an inconvenient truth for those hoping for a fullness of life characterised by amazing deeds for us to do that make the adventure simply about a glowing 'us'.

My first surgery was made more poignant by the expectation of success through the eyes of my daughter. Playmobil again, this time a scene visualising the operation with me lying in bed and my consultant holding the removed cavernoma (modelled by a raisin) aloft with oversized plastic tongs. The whole family were gathered as figurines sellotaped to cardboard, and she had done what children (and athletes) do; visualised success – a happy ending. It impacted me so much that I took a photo of the carefully balanced gathering, but it didn't occur like that in reality and as a family we consequently had to walk towards more unknowns. Yes, I felt angry, perhaps more so because I wanted God to be straightforwardly good in response to her best imaginings.

With the disappointments of illness, trauma or life-changing circumstances shaping my understanding of a fullness of life, by now you probably have me pigeon-holed as a negative liberal spoiling the evangelical party. Instead, I request your understanding that rather than spoiling it, I am actually finding a better reason to celebrate, discovering for myself through unconventional means that Jesus has matters in hand. I am moving towards a more tangible, rusted cross of Christ instead of varnished pine, its rough splintered wood pointing towards an honesty of life which remains within the scope of life in all its fullness. Accepting that knowing Christ may involve suffering is surely the honest beginnings of an eternal life, both in quality and time, because the dominance of fear is removed, both now and continuing. Real fullness of life sweeps up suffering, embracing it, turning it into something we could never imagine, where battle lines fall, defences are exposed and our vocabulary for God broadens as he dwells within our 'taking part'. I know it from these stroke years, from hospital conversations where I was as free as a bird, having been reminded of my vulnerability. Simone Weil once suggested that affliction actually manifests

God's presence uniquely instead of disproving it.[7] And, for me at least, illness has made God more alive than I could have ever imagined.

Note too that what we regard as health and illness in our society are themselves often upside down. Jesus once commented that it was only the sick who needed a doctor,[8] beautifully provocative as he again challenged the self-perceptions of the healthy righteous. Affluence, including health, can deter us from him as we aspire to what we believe will be the 'whole life'. Malcolm Muggeridge discovered this during a three-week documentary filming an enclosed religious order in a Cistercian Abbey at Nunraw, Scotland, where the monks appeared to be depriving themselves of a complete experience of life, at least in terms of sensual satisfaction. However, they shone an extraordinary peace, compared to the symptoms and complaints of those who live within an affluent society.[9] We all arrive at this conclusion one way or another, and the sooner the better. I always suspected affluence to fall short, perhaps because I've always had food to eat, a roof over my head and the greatest of luxuries – choice. But I have certainly known poverty of spirit too where the hunger for God and the desire to set faith free, like a greyhound from its trap, have become a nagging deprivation of the populist 'whole life' pursuit. This, in God's eyes, must be our deepest sickness.

I dream for the church to embody this upturned remedy, where *taking part is truly winning*; a community which is diverse yet unifying, welcoming and sending, empathising and enabling, accepting yet transformational, inclusive of those who tried to do amazing things for God yet exclusively about a God who amazes us once we've blown it. A familiar place (with a history and perception hard to shake), yet a hive of momentum and an organic future. An imaginative A&E where the openly sick delve deeper into fullness of life, where all unite and take part around agreed sacraments; around the cross.

Does my own experience of the all-embracing fullness of life and consequent dreams for church remove all doubt? No, fear still shows its head and hope will probably tussle with faith for all my life. Here again, running marathons reminds me of suffering's quiet fear, the unusual duration and distance one faces, the physical and mental journey to which only participants can testify (even though some believe that once you have run one marathon, 'you always have it in your legs'). But like Paul, having suffering 'in my legs' can only lead to knowing more of Christ, and running's physical movement still excites me because it's a choice of how to invest my life, my time, my body, and now I've tasted the rich cordial of faith and hope, I pursue it.

The joys and the sufferings of my running experiences have helped me to explain how hope and faith create this wonderful trajectory onwards, the happy ending of taking part *now*. I have shared my difficult times, and like regrets – regrets which become iron bars surrounding our lives and inhibiting our personalities – there is a way through. Our next chapter finds a group of men paralysed by their pasts, the blue-clad hardened prisoners of the Oregon State Penitentiary, USA, who know how it feels to need a way forward. Like me, they fear the wall, only theirs is concrete and 14ft high. That wall must stop them from seeing physical sunsets and dreaming of happy endings, but guess what? Taking part in running is their way through it.

11

When Hope and Love Speak to Each Other

I do not run like someone running aimlessly; I do not fight like a boxer beating the air.[1]

There is so much to say about the connection between hope and love, or in my case, temporary disability and running. People run for many reasons and it means rehabilitation for many of us, restoring us to fitter bodies and healthier minds. No distance runners run aimlessly; at least, you wouldn't follow such an isolated discipline for long without discovering a worthwhile reason to lace up during an icy December and get out of the door before daylight. I choose to do it because I know I'm at my best when running is in my life, socially and personally. I think more clearly, make better decisions and mentally stocktake my priorities. I suppose I run towards a better 'me' and when I was ill it provided a target for recovery.

The Oregon State Penitentiary, located an hour south of Portland, USA, is an astonishingly poignant symbol of the restorative nature of running. Monthly 5 and 10k races see the male-only inmates compete against each other and there is also the Annual High Wall Half Marathon, needing thirty-one loops of the 2,250ft-long prison yard to complete the distance. It sounds monotonous, of course, but therein lies the power of running: not to forget about our circumstances but to cope with them, to continue living with them. Those square laps under the sun's heat are steps of hope and running is loved by inmates; it stops them fighting their lives; beating the air.

Things we love often create hope, but I am aware that exercise which provides a pleasurable escape can also take over one's life and become an addiction. But, as I will say many times, running is not my God nor does it take precedence over other aspects of my life; sometimes my children need me, my wife needs me, sometimes there are just more pressing things to do. Running in itself gives me no permanent hope as I know that as my body ages, one day my speed will reduce and there will not be another race. When our recreation begins to control our behaviour, or we suddenly find our right-minded priorities in an unfamiliar order, we are in trouble. The rock band U2 summed this up with a song describing the desperate story of two people caught in a cycle of heroin addiction, running whilst their circumstances remained stationary.[2] This is all we are doing if the buzz from running[3] is the goal of the chase, but running is a discipline for me, like prayer or reading the Bible, through which I can become more open, receptive and finally cooperate with God.

Inside the high-walled Oregon prison yard, we find a miracle of wholeness and restoration at work. Most beautiful to me is the invitation for men and women from the outside to join these races, running alongside the inmates, in a wonderful snapshot of togetherness, or of hope and love at a dinner date. It's no secret that we are all prisoners inside our own walls, whether you have acknowledged yours yet or not, and therefore this 'alongside-ness', this 'being with' has experienced increased interest from outside runners since the prison was featured in *Runner's World* magazine in June 2015.[4] The running club itself, organised by inmates, has a waiting list of longer than a year because only 130 prisoners out of 2,000 are able to take part and joining requires eighteen months of good behaviour. In this programme I see humanity coming to terms with itself, honestly deciding to move forward instead of throwing the static strop of fighting 'like a boxer beating the air'.

It is also clear that some people run 'from' and others run 'to'. The past, present and future hang, like confined nicotine, in the air of this prison. Prisoners run from their histories, the stress of being in jail and to participate in some kind of normal, healthy activity.[5] These dimensions of past, normalisation in the present and facing the future, characterise hope in the light of love. Togetherness in running physically manifests a healing of spirit and rehabilitation of individuals. This is partly why I love it.

I cannot fully appreciate the impact of this club upon the perpetrators of violent crimes because, of course, I am on the outside, but I can share in the meditative quality of our sport. When I train for a spring marathon through the winter, I am very aware of temperature and conditions underfoot, so hat and gloves feature in my kit. I breathe a cloud of smoke as I begin, aware of the cold, but after a few minutes of focus upon my breathing, lowering my arms and picking up my cadence, I become less aware of my body and increasingly notice the dawn with its emerging colours of first light. I raise my head, which until this point has fixated my eyes upon the rolling pavement (a personal weakness of mine is that I know I need to look further into the distance with a better angle). I then begin to feel relaxed, checking my Garmin for my pace, and achieve the feeling of being more present as I cut through the surrounding air whose temperature is no longer my foe. I frequently wipe a tear from my left eye (for some reason this tear duct is very active when I run on colder days) as a smile spreads across my face, taking in the Dickensian sight of streetlights and smoke billowing from chimneys or from vents as central heating systems cough into life. As for me, I feel a little smug, thrilled to be warm and efficient in the early morning fog of the quiet Ashford streets; the best place on earth, right there, right then.

I sometimes think of the Oregon runners as I run meditatively. They do laps of the prison yard with the sun beating down, each time the prison wall providing a haven of shade for a few seconds, temporary relief from the blistering heat. I love the way they sometimes track back and pick up slower finishers, holding up the hands at the finishing line of those about to be released that are running in the yard for the final time. This unique club speaks to me about encouraging others and coming alongside the suffering; love providing hope and hope manifested as love. I often wish that churches demonstrated this more, ditching our eagerness to tidy away and allowing togetherness to have its way, slowing down to be there for the least, casting aside our veneer and admitting that this life can be tough; true freedom surely lies in celebrating the real stories of real people. Anything less and church becomes another prison.

Inside Oregon, people cannot hide their imprisoned status. The real miracle that takes place is that the runners learn to love their wounds, almost miss them. The symbol of his fourteen-year detainment, the high wall was transformed from enemy into friend for Kelley Slayton when he returned to run there after being released in 2006.[6]

This is redemption, when something destructive and designed to restrict becomes transformed into a symbol of creativity and freedom. We don't get many opportunities in life to look back and value the tougher times, we're too busy moving on and papering them over, but Kelley Slayton knows the power of resurrection over death through running.

Having highlighted some of the reasons people run, I need to applaud a movement which I regard as prophetic in embodying hope's chemistry with love. I often show up in the early hours of a weekend to see the same regular faces; a committed team of volunteers giving up their time to set up and steward an event that means so much to so many people. The air thick with expectation, conversation buds into life amongst this community. Our group is diverse in age, colour and dress code. There are families, couples, children, grandchildren, grandparents, those with pushchairs and dogs on leads. Some arrivals sip water, while headphones assist others with a pick-me-up. I hear laughter because these people like being together, and they are only silenced by a voice on the hour who stands to announce that we may begin. First-timers are welcomed with applause by the faithful and the wooden platform upon which our leader stands is not the pulpit of a church, but a park bench – welcome to 'Parkrun'.

Parkrun was the brainchild of Paul Sinton-Hewitt CBE, who ran in his local park in 2004 with the idea of getting people together to run 5k each week demanding no financial cost, just their time. Ten years later it had surpassed the 1 million participants mark, and he was honoured by the Queen for services to grass roots sports participation. Parkrun is accessible for every age and ability; some runners chase the thrill of a new PB while others celebrate getting to the starting line while the clock still reads a.m.! Parkrun has snowballed worldwide and I am thankful for what it has reminded me about grass roots church. Because when I see the exhausted-looking man dressed in his 1980s headband, gasping, red-faced, pushing himself towards the finishing line to the encouragements of his local community, my emotions are stirred. He is neither first nor last, but affirmed. His kit is not from the Nike store, he has probably never been to one, but this store of friendship satisfies him and lifts me too. The dog-walkers and pram-pushers arrive home as well, applauded in their unorthodox achievement, though normal here.

Taking my place as a runner amidst this traffic, with stewards restoring my bearings and sometimes my son pushing me onwards with his own aspirations, both of us feeling so alive, there is no place I'd rather be. It challenges me and speaks about forgiveness; there are people I know, have worked with, people who don't know I know them, or don't remember me. People whose lives have seen traumas of divorce, bereavements or bad business decisions; an entire soap opera is running, different from running with strangers because I am tempted to judge them because I have knowledge of what they are running 'from' and what they are running 'to'. Some here would even admit to running to stand still. But I cannot judge, because God reminds me that we're all running and that the lie of the land around the cross is level.

This audacious leveller, Parkrun, creates the sparks of love and hope meeting once again. We're back in the present, and for a moment I've hung up my warped obsession for Christianity to be about happy endings. No emerald cities for green-faced finishers; just life, just running, just a road with twists and turns for brainless scarecrows like me. As someone who loves the church and longs for it to mirror the alternative community only Jesus creates, Parkrun speaks to me. Within this increasing fold which loves the least, the lost and the last (there is always a tail-walker so that the most sheepish are never left alone), I believe that something subtle is informing the church here, like an early church to which God 'added to their number daily'.[7] The week I first wrote these words, 8,325 people across the UK competed in their first ever Parkrun.

But by now you know that Slayton is not the only one in prison, so let me tell you about the family holiday which only truly got started when we boarded the pedalo. We'd been tolerating each other during the six-hour drive down to the French campsite but frustrations had remained unspoken. The four of us had been immersed in our own lives of work and school up until this point, juggling pressures and expectations, yet not finding the place to voice them. We'd argue over first-world problems, the salt and pepper, the football sock that had not reached the laundry bin, the drama of fitting the roof rack with little offer of support. But as we stepped onto the bobbing blue lake, glistening under a beaming Vendée sunshine, we were all captive inside our hired red craft for the next hour.

Creeping away from the jetty, two of us immediately pedalled like crazy and we didn't seem to move terribly far. The other two took over and still nothing. I began a breathing routine much like on a tempo run,[8] at about 80 per cent effort capacity, pumping my legs, determined to get us at least moving, being proud of my fitness and obsession to succeed. I was like a lost man without a map, beating the air. Other pedalo users in the distance seemed to have it nailed; they were even enjoying it, finding respite to look up and point out details on the surrounding hillsides, trees, cottages, sometimes pointing at us and our daft craft. I was furiously confined in our plastic prison. We eventually discovered that the less frantically we pedalled, the greater our momentum until, forced into slowness, I found that the experience actually became enjoyable. Once accustomed to the rhythms of the water and the milder wash we were creating (to the approval of nearby fishermen), we settled into pedalo pace and everybody breathed. It was as if those first ten minutes reflected the dysfunctional spin we had wrapped ourselves into as a family, and now, in the calm sloshing of water against boat, we could at last address the pressing issues.

I laughed inwardly at our turbulent start, before commencing my classic Dad routine. With no sympathy for rudeness from children, I kicked things off with some general remarks along the lines of: 'So, what's got into you recently? I don't know who taught you to speak like that. This cannot go on . . . ' Perhaps not the greatest of holiday openers, but I knew nobody could escape, no doors could be slammed and we were too far from the bank for anyone to paddle off. There followed lots of laughter and bouncing around, like a lid released on a can of tennis balls. I cannot remember much about the next half an hour, but I do know that by the time we stepped off we were bonded as a family and a lot of meaningful talking had taken place. We had addressed what needed airing and everyone had taken their opportunity; in emotional terms we were back on an even keel. (I had a momentary secret swell of Dad pride, a head-festival that the hiring of the boat had delivered way more than our few euros' worth.) In keeping with the lush green and blue of hills and sky reflecting in the water, we had been brought to look at ourselves and eventually laugh at our foolish ways, our misunderstandings of one another, our misreading of situations. We were free.

The creation of an honest space to vent emotions is one benefit I derive from running; it's just me listening to my legs, my chest, my burning throat, feeling every muscle twinge and every stitch. There is nowhere to hide and I open up, relishing this moment. I suppose I could stop and walk home if it hurt, but I'm headstrong and that is never going to happen with me. I pulled up once after a hard hill effort at night in the pouring rain, when it felt like my calf muscles were bursting out of my skin. I carried calf supports in my waterproof jacket back then, slipped them on, and continued my training. I tend to push and push, harder and harder. In my right mind, I am aware of the irresponsibility of this, leaving myself spent for the rest of the day if I have truly paced out early in the morning, often with a list of DIY tasks as long as my laces left undone. My dear wife is patient with this patient, but I do it because I can talk to God through this level of focus.

Sometimes, this pain can feel like an act of penance for the many times I've let God down in my life. Truly, I often tell him this on my runs, saying his name between gasps over and over, wondering if my life would bear more fruit if I had made other choices. Sometimes I wonder where I'd be if I hadn't walked away from the fire. But happily, guilt and running hard have not proved to be a simultaneous equation; I never feel or hear any negative response from God to my running honesty; just joy, like a child at play, and I have learned that I need this time.

All my complex solutions are futile when my exhausted body reminds me of my limits and of God's grace which saves me from my self-importance. It reminds me that I need not put things right because in his eyes they already are, and one can only start from here. Like Kelley's prison yard and the pedalo, the limits of our effort are the start of our salvation because this look in the mirror reveals that illness is deeper than physical. It's often about painful memories and wanting justice, or about self-worth and the question of: do I really matter? Running has shown me this illness of desiring significance and although I cannot remedy every fault I find, at least I become aware of them; my selfish motives, my narcissistic hopes and my deepest fears. These are addressed by Paul's triangle of love (which cautions my motives), hope (which puts my hopes back in God and not myself) and faith (which rebukes my fears). Passing drivers, some occasionally honking their horns (I probably taught their children, or I may have taught *them*!), would not have a clue about my running discourse, my attempted deals with God. A phrase I once heard in Christian circles was the idea of 'doing business with God', but I think God doing business with me is a much healthier transaction. The initiative of grace is always his, so the content of my running consciousness comes from him – the revelations in thought, the noticing of beauty, my gratitude for family and friends.

I wonder if this honest exchange (which I see as prayer) and the salvific nature of running is down to the simple mechanics of the biological process? Running involves inhaling oxygen and absorbing it into the bloodstream through the lungs, which is then carried to the muscles. Training increases the efficiency of this continuous oxygenation process. The strengthened heart pumps a greater volume of blood and so needs to beat less often when at rest. The volume of air taken in, the rate of process through the lungs and the circulatory system carrying oxygenated blood to muscle tissues is constantly improving.[9] I feel switched on and more alive, physically and spiritually, because there is no easy way round it; if you want to run you need to train and if I want to become a Christian with a stronger heart, I'm going to have to work at it, particularly with the respiration of prayer.

But my heart doesn't always host a positive view of others, or increasing capacity to love. In truth, I don't always like what running has shown me, but by going to extremes of physical exhaustion I often end up in a more receptive state along the way. Vanity, ego, whatever you name it, have always been close to the surface of my personality. Runners know that looking over your shoulder can be a huge mistake and sign of weakness; you need to keep your own pace and run your own race while the rest of the field run theirs, and when I was in the midst of Bible college I did my best to temper it, despite constant affirmations of my ability to lead musical worship, to communicate creatively or being perceived as a future principal or by my tutor as 'a man of God'. I've now lived ten silent years without standing in such public roles, but the wilderness has been necessary.

I soon knew my arrogance after leaving the fire and was watching colleagues from afar, who I then realised were the true people of God digging away in their local communities to make a kingdom difference, one anonymous encounter at a time. I recorded these words to God in my journal on 7 April 2010:

My Officership found its value in relation to other Officers, those whom I was better than, more eloquent or more creative. Today, they turn this around; they have developed, shown faith, lived as committed servants in ways I fell short, so I am ashamed of my pride, reliance upon intellect and secret desire to upstage them. This journey has revealed my error, a need for status, and now broken, having become nothing, I learn that you alone deserve the credit for all ministries.

Those Officers were the real heroes, still serving God and humanity without checking over their shoulders. As I conclude this uncomfortable chapter, I am grateful that the crucible of running draws my prejudices and limitations to the surface, and although the blue line took me on a difficult route, it is good to finally accept that I cannot win every race. Falling from our best-laid plans and then letting God work on us is when faith often begins.

My Officer friend/pacemaker Gordon did once admit that he might not cope too well if there was nobody to listen to his opinions. I was relieved to hear this from such an exemplary man, because there still remains a small part of me that craves significance; it's probably in you too? This was certainly true for one first-time marathoner Bill Crotty watched by his wife, for whom the experience gave her a lump in the throat and formed a tear in her eye. Bill didn't beat many others but that was never his aim. He beat the marathon and that prize is his forever.[10] This dad who initiates the pedalo conversations, who wants to take control, seeking my moment in the sun and doing well at something; perhaps this is why others chase a marathon place too and this is our moment of coming together pounding London's streets, though none of us really want to admit it? We all experience obstacles in life, and maybe the marathon gives us a concrete metaphor where our ability to overcome them becomes obvious for all to see? I can appreciate that mountain-conquering completeness of passing under that final London Marathon digital clock knowing that the mission is complete, tears in my eyes, euphoria running through my veins. I haven't found it anywhere else in life, but I imagine meeting Jesus will be like that.

Yet in the meantime there will be other missions, more subtle, less loud and often private. I now see a story arc here, but it is quite the opposite of turning into a superhero who conquers the world. Of course, I miss the days when my children would bound up to me after a day's work like a dog greeting its owner through the front door. I might crave the box of fireworks released to celebrate my return, but I'm afraid that ageing robs this away all too soon. I still want to make them proud and I guess tying things up for me means running, especially after illness, getting back to my best and giving them that picture. The American George Sheehan, not just running's doctor but thought of as its reigning philosopher, once likened sport to a dramatic stage on which a saint could be made from a sinner and an uncommon hero be made of a common man.[11] And as a husband and father, I recognise my desire to become an uncommon hero once in a while. Yes, this can be as futile as beating the air and I admit that this *is* the heart of illness, because I know that hope and love do not always end so neatly, which is when only faith is able to provide the last word. How fascinating that the interplay of these two elements exposes the need for the third.

12

When Love and Faith Speak to Each Other

I press on towards the goal to win the prize for which God has called me heavenwards in Christ Jesus.[1]

Running is a lesson in anonymity; it's just me and the streets, uncomplicated, straightforward. Apart from the big races, you don't often hear anyone else's encouragement. This is just what I need in my life right now; it may be my life stage, but I must live with not being in the spotlight. This makes the experience more authentic but equally, I feel more introverted about fullness of life than ever before; I don't shout about it, but there is certainly a calling inside. The Christian evangelists would panic at my admission, 'Whatever happened to mission, going into all the world and making disciples?',[2] but let me unpack this with reflection upon a faith which has learned some tough lessons and now ricochets back to me from a place of love.

My early faith days were dangerous. I had the news that would change the world, but not always the tact or the relationships; many times I tried to drive the articulated lorry of salvation over the rope bridge of casual acquaintances. I listened to preachers, I read the books, I learned about 'warm areas' and evangelistic strategies. Then one day, one of my most influential college Bible teachers, a pace-setter and humble figure of immense spiritual insight who quite simply loves Jesus, encouraged my insight into the inauthenticity of forming friendships just to make people into Christians when he asked, how would I feel if an atheist befriended me just so that I might become an atheist? Only a few years into the journey of faith and I had, sadly, already begun to see people purely as 'souls', targets, data.

Still today, I notice this tension raise its head, that of growth versus depth, which for leaders committed to Christlike love-driven authenticity can become as draining as 'splat the rat'. I still have not unwrapped the golden ticket for growing the body of Christ outwards, but I unfortunately have learned many ways of how to make it die inwards.

However, I believe that diversity is part of the solution. A few months ago, I was running early one morning and passed through an industrial park which spreads either side of a wide road on the outskirts of Ashford. In our town is a large Nepalese community who appear to understand the secrets behind the benefits of rising early, so I often jog past them, raising my hand and saying 'good morning' as they nod their heads, husbands walking a few metres ahead of their wives as seems to be the custom. This particular morning was the first time I had seen a Nepalese runner, fairly well-built but never before seen on my regular 8-mile circuit. He was wearing all-black kit, and was on the same side of the road as me as we ran towards each other. Late on, I realised he had headphones in so I simply raised my hand holding my water bottle – my companion on hundreds of runs, since a disturbing experience of losing energy miles from home and having to stop at a garage to buy some Lucozade. I was calm, doing my normal thing, but he on the other hand was pumped, not just in physique, but mentally. I don't know if his music had transported him to somewhere far from Ashford but he gave the loudest 'Good morning!' with smile that I've ever run into. Well-meant, of course, but it felt like overkill as his voice bounced off the walls of the B&Q warehouse and echoed around the street, which was otherwise silent. I laughed to myself as God reminded me of my early days of belief, and that there are good and bad ways of 'pressing on' in faith.

If I'm really honest, my misguided evangelical crusade also made *me* look good (image, as I've highlighted earlier in this book, being something that running has begun to free me from). I began to focus too much on being like the preacher, instead of being like Christ, preoccupied with influence and plaudits from the pews. I first became aware of this distorted self-seeking faith, when writers challenged me, like Oswald Chambers did with: 'The true character of the loveliness that tells for God is always unconscious. Conscious influence is priggish and un-Christian.'[3] I became too aware of doing good works, demonstrating love like clumsy fingers grab a butterfly, at which point you have crushed the very thing itself. I guess the only way out of this is to live fully in the present (as we have seen running facilitates), just as young children, blissfully unaware, demonstrate in their play.

But even when you want your faith to make you a star, God seems to have the last word – love breaks through and he takes 'playing at love' and transforms it into a lesson in love. When I was a member of The Salvation Army in central London, our church often engaged with the homeless community, ever present on the streets. I met a man, a few years older than me, who had come to the church for help and with whom I ended up building a good friendship. I had enjoyed a privileged up-bringing, but he opened my eyes to life on the other side of the street.

There was the time I visited him in a hotel room facing one of London's beautiful parks where he had temporarily been housed by the council, and I cannot forget the scars he showed me along his arm, ripped open and brutal as he disclosed another attempt at suicide. The learning curve was steep for me, and I remember how angry I felt when I returned to the pristine church that evening where I would sing and play music of a love that provides hope for such as he. I now know the anger was my inability to square the circle, to reconcile my life and his. But my theories of life in all its fullness were being truly shaken.

One of the final times I saw him was when I received a phone call to say that he had again attempted to take his own life, this time with a heroin overdose, another person running to stand still. He was brain-damaged and being treated in St Thomas' Hospital opposite the River Thames. With no family, no next of kin, I arrived to find this man lying on a mattress directly on the floor, unable to speak or pretty much do anything for himself. I wanted to cry. I don't know how I got through that visit, standing there in my suit after work, but I just spoke to him while the nurses stared at me, reassuring him that I was there and that there were people who cared. My faith was being stirred and my predictable outcomes were quickly becoming irrelevant; there are no means of measuring the impact of anonymous love.

As I look back on those moments from more than twenty years ago, I begin to see how they changed me, not in the sense of making me look better or earn God's favour, but reducing me to a helpless state of disbelief when confronted with injustice for the first time. This was no longer a performance; all I had to give was love and the only outlet where I could direct my anger was God, perhaps the church. Raging against love and needing more of it. Something boils up at such times, a seed is sown, and you never want to settle for faith without love ever again. Getting rid of frustrations and allowing love to break into my life is partly why I run. I need to breathe out the waste and breathe in the good, exhale my questions and inhale God.

I still have so far to go, not in distance but in character. Can love emerge from my ego-project of forty years plus so that my life can be a pointer towards God? Love seems so anti-me; it does not crave the mic, is not painted in the brightest colours, it arrives and departs unannounced. But when it draws along-side you, you know you've seen it, felt it, received it because it remains attractive in the silence of memory, long after the applause has rippled its last. It's not Damascus but Emmaus, remember, where the disciples took time to know it.

I don't think the recalibration process would be so success-ful if I didn't listen to music on my runs, and my experience of fullness of life has always benefited from soundtracks. I'm definitely a closet charismatic, often criticised for not being de-monstrative enough in church services which cannot always be expected to excite or energise everyone. Admittedly, my heart-beat (which rests at thirty-nine beats per minute whereas the average is between sixty and ninety) is very slow. In hospital, the staff taking my blood pressure always comment upon it, asking, 'Do you run?' I'm quite proud of my athlete's pulse, even more so when I found out that Naoko Takahashi, gold medallist at the Sydney Olympics, has a pulse of thirty-five. So, with this slow heartbeat I run to maintain my faith. The times when I *am* charismatic and punch the air (sometimes causing passing drivers to bib their horns at this unorthodox jogger behaviour) are normally when I have just listened to a sermon podcast and I am celebrating along with my music, thankful for not another shaved split time but a fresh insight into God! As I listen and reflect upon the mutual exchange between faith and love – fullness of life and running – running becomes a sermon in footsteps for me.

I never use music on race days because I want to be in the moment and absorb the energy of the spectators, but it has been a big part of my running life since 2012, assisting my mental stamina to fight the monotony of solitary runs lasting for hours. Nothing beats the transition from a concluding 'Amen' into a track such as Marlena Shaw's 1969 'California Soul' or the inspirational complexity of Donald Fagen's 2012 modestly jubilant 'I'm Not the Same Without You'. This latter example from the Steely Dan frontman is a song about recovery from failed love and appropriately mirrors what I am trying to describe in this chapter, leaving toxic influences behind. Music for me is like passing a refreshment station; it somehow gives my steps a lift, which I've often needed when glycogen goes low and I am caught out miles from home. I don't always run in time with it, in fact there was one occasion in mid-July where I got my playlist mixed up and was jogging to 'Away in a Manger' sung by St Paul's Cathedral choir. The people at the bus stop I passed would have had no idea about the bizarreness of my private world at that moment, reminding me that in running there is always a funny side.

My favourite song when training for my 2012 marathon became The Pretenders' 'Don't Get Me Wrong' from 1986. It has a background guitar riff which always lifted my cadence and became so much part of my training that when I hear that song now, I picture running and pavements passing underfoot.

I have already highlighted 'Running Up That Hill' by Kate Bush, released in 1985, which always makes me think of the biblical Abraham, firewood strapped to his back, climbing to a place to sacrifice his son Isaac. Interestingly, a version of this same song was used during the closing ceremony of the 2012 London Olympics prior to the presentation of medals for the marathon.

More recently, during my recovery from surgery I have been finding songs for my next running playlist which will certainly include 'Purple Rain' by the late artist Prince. The music conveys something which words cannot express about love speaking to faith. The guitar set-up is so overdriven and at such high volume that the entire track has a pregnancy about it, a tension just hanging in the air, Prince's guitar feeding back and wanting to scream like a greyhound on a lead. Fullness of life is like that for me, pregnant with hope, and infused with a subconscious love. Prince's guitar expresses the angst that I have felt in living my faith authentically. I cannot wait to run to this track because I am bound to feel emotional. I feel very blessed to have been able to listen to more music through running because God uses it to speak to me when I have not heard him through other means in life.

I wanted this chapter to outline the conversation that occurs between love and faith (my running and believing in God), and I have learned two specific things; that fullness of life demands a context (faith requires love) and secondly, that love requires faith if it is to persist, shining through the clouds. I would like to explain this mutual dependence with two final metaphors.

Faith requires love. There was one winter where it snowed and the pavements were hazardous, leading me to break one of my rules about running and head for the gym. I don't get on with treadmills and being inside, the experience feels artificial – I need to be outside and feel the wind on my face. My belief, therefore, needs a context, it cannot be stored as theory upon theory which only leads to spiritual obesity. A boring run; I never went back to the gym.

As an outdoors-only runner I have also seen a lot of skies. I tend to marvel upwards much of the time, especially in winter when I put the bins out and gaze at the dazzling array of stars above me, emerging all the more the longer you look upwards. The skies remind me, thanks to the world of cinema, that faith needs expression through love and love requires faith: Batman's yellow bat signal has become an image projected onto clouds telling Gotham City that he is needed and present. I like the bat signal shape, which can only be seen due to cloud cover acting as a backdrop, otherwise the light beams would continue infinitely with no form. For me, the cross of Christ is my bat signal, where light met with time, hitting earth 2,000 years ago. God and love have always been there somewhere in my thinking, but it's only when they encountered the clouds I have described in this book that this love was revealed to be cruciform in shape; a suffering love, and potentially a suffering faith.

On Wednesday 9 August 2017, Botswana's Isaac Makwala ran a 200m time trial at the World Athletics Championships in the London Stadium. After being officially withdrawn through a suspected outbreak of the norovirus one day earlier, Makwala was reinstated and successfully sped home in 20.20 seconds to qualify for the semifinals. Incredibly, he ran that race solo and I was there. The cheers of the crowd were deafening and I had a lump in my throat seeing a single figure speed around the bend, roared on by a crowd cheering for just one man. I will probably never experience anything like it in an athletics stadium ever again, but God spoke to me through it; exile exchanged for welcome, illness for triumph. Makwala stuck to his lane, forgetting the distractions and media attention of the past twenty-four hours, and fuelled by a one-ness within that stadium, he simply did the job and ran home. That is all I need to do; the rest of the field is not my concern; love as the force behind me and faith the finishing line ahead of me.

Love is purity of purpose, love is disinfected intent, pressing on through faith in Christ. I'm not there yet, but the things I love are transforming me and God is moulding me, chiselling away at my character, nurturing my faith through this spiritual discipline of running.

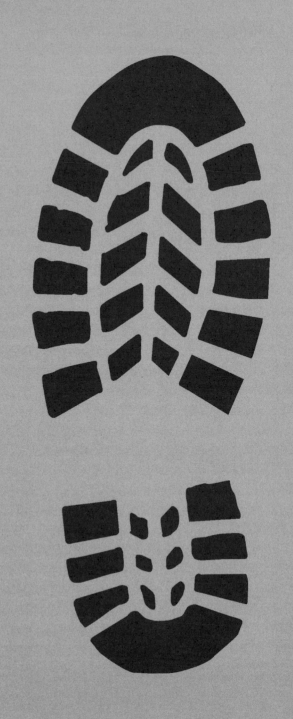

13

Ever Present

I have fought the good fight, I have finished the race, I have kept the faith.[1]

Marathon running is as much about getting to the starting line on Blackheath as it is about finishing on The Mall. The months of preparation are fraught with the pitfalls of injury, the balancing of training and resting, and hopefully the gradual increase of self-belief that a person can go the whole distance; training holds many battles which seem insignificant to the non-runner. The challenge still has a certain aura about it and we finishers are proudly in the minority of the population. However, I hope this book has not just been about running, but has shone a light upon going the whole distance in life, because our outlook on God, our self-worth, our relationships past, present and future, determine whether we make the starting line of our tomorrows. I have shared some of my 'race' with you, the reader, and you will know by now that there have been moments of 'fight' as my discernment of God's character has rebounded within the triangle of faith, hope and love. His presence has very much been tested through the darker times, and the reflecting challenge for me has been to engage with life as it stands, now, not life 'one day' when health is consistent. *I* need to become ever present too.

I was thrilled when one of my vulnerabilities, the power of the mind, which often prevents my ever-presence, became the focus of a BBC documentary in April 2017. *Mind Over Marathon* featured a group of ten amateur runners living with different mental health issues, and shadowed them through their London Marathon training as they confronted lives defined by challenges including anxiety or post-traumatic stress disorder. Running for Heads Together, the Official Charity of the Year for the 2017 race, they were supported by the Duke and Duchess of Cambridge and HRH Prince Harry in an attempt to remove the stigma surrounding mental health issues.

I rarely watch television (I'm either writing, reading, running or playing my guitar), but tears came to my eyes as I listened to their stories, saw their frailty and empathised with the apparent salvation these people had found in running. I knew something of what they were describing; the sense of vitality it brings, the joy of community, the strong bond of friendships, the awareness of love. I was further delighted when my local church featured a clip of this programme in one of its services, because the connection between running and what I look upon as a kind of 'presence spirituality' (which I have long-suspected personally) was recognised by an audience that may have missed the documentary, especially when Christianity comes across as preoccupied with pearly gates or confines discipleship to more traditional spiritual disciplines. I just love God's surprises. He is surely in all things!

I now want to talk about looking ahead, and this final chapter to be a signpost. I am grateful that you have stayed with me as I have tried to describe my life of running and believing within the triangle of faith, hope and love. Constantly bringing me back to my three significant reference points, fullness of life, illness and running, I now see that the Tempro line of believing in God along the road has meanderings and hidden dangers, and so will yours. Surely it is better to count this cost at the outset than begin only to hit the wall? Marathons require dedication and endurance, so make sure that this is what you are signing up for. If you can get to see it amongst the crowd, the broken blue line is not a straightforward path, so make sure you want it. It might lead you through suffering and it may lead you through joy, but I hope that my own particular route has created a more real, resilient and enduring passage for your doubt and belief.

Like you, I frequently see news images of flash floods around our climate-changing planet, and I am, though not proud of it, virtually immune to footage of families scrambling between rooftops by shuffling along a thin rope to safety. Maybe this book has thrown you a lifeline – you were in the sunshine of fullness of life before tragedy struck, and now you are up to your neck in a storm. Helicopters don't carry everyone out, and I've wanted my analysis of the tension that exists between hope and fullness of life to burst that bubble and replace it with a permanent blue line that gets us across this flood. Unlike temporary Tempro, which is eventually washed away, the rope withstanding the flood's force emphasises the truth for me that God cannot have temporary characteristics, but is to be known in a way that outgrows fleeting highs and childish ways. His permanence draws out my hunger; his ever-presence calling me towards mine.

This is because the crucified God in Christ, a one-ness many would rather separate, allows me to exercise my freedom – to run to or from him; the absorption and transformation of all my fickle humanity. Writer Pete Greig, author, pastor and founder of the 24-7 Prayer movement alludes to this when reflecting upon the story of Adam and Eve: 'God created for them the dangerous possibility of disobedience in order to create the higher possibility of voluntary submission . . . God made humanity to share in the very exquisite relationship of mutual self-sacrifice that exists at the heart of His being.'[2] The vulnerability of the running God is a staggering truth of Christianity but a sure-footed claim upon my life.

This book has come to show that the self-sacrificing broken blue line of God is therefore the way of love. 'God is love',[3] so love is God. The romantic, loving wedding promises we began with require much striving on our part – I am not *patient* when I follow my wife wandering around IKEA or when she thinks of the next DIY task. I try yet fail not to keep 'a record of wrongs'[4] while she is driving (as I continue becoming accustomed to my year as a passenger on medical grounds!). When we strive we fail; instead, these Corinthian adjectives are ever-present attributes of God – kindness, 'does not envy' nor 'boast', 'is not proud', 'is not self-seeking', 'is not easily angered', 'rejoices with the truth', 'protects', 'trusts', 'hopes' and 'perseveres'.[5] When we receive them as a description of God, we are swept into the arms of a running Father who graciously welcomes returning prodigals at his own initiative. As I have already pointed out, running for me is a discipline but it acts as a dispenser of this grace; I receive it through my three-fold commitment of mind, heart and will. The need to be ever present in mind, heart and will was echoed by Dr Martyn Lloyd-Jones's warning about 'will' only people 'who decide to take up Christianity instead of being taken up by Christianity.'[6] Swept up, free from striving, grace sums up every benefit I enjoy from running.

Looking ahead but aware of this danger, I will continue to live out my belief in God within the tension of my triangle, never forgetting that I am a brain-weary scarecrow in need of his healing of past, present and future. This book has tried to explain that each element moulds the next, rubs off the edges, refines them through experience. I want 'the greatest of these',[7] love, to continue to inform my approach to future suffering (hope) and future fullness of life (faith). As they do, I commit to remaining ever present in each encounter with others and in the streets through which I run.

I've kept these three terms somewhat limited to what they mean to me as a runner and hospital patient – they are likely to mean something different for you. I have not cross-referenced them or delved into Greek meanings, just taken them at face value for their immediate accessibility and how they speak to me today. If I've got them wrong, please don't put me in a theological camp; fundamentalists fighting liberals and vice versa is a dull war, as is an evangelical Christian trying to convert the running community. This was never my aim. I have ricocheted between them, but I'm still here, I'm still running, and I'm a runner who believes in God, or perhaps a Christian who believes in running.

Given the nature of this book, chiefly to shine a light upon God's ever-presence throughout my own battles with strokes and the widening lens of fullness of life, it is appropriate in this final chapter to give a standing ovation to a group of runners who are my inspiration. They are the 'Ever Presents', originally consisting of forty-two members who were formally acknowledged by the organisers of the London Marathon after fifteen years, who took part in the first event in 1981 and are still

running it today. Thirty-nine marathons later, with the passing
of time, joints and lives weathered by storms of circumstance,
as I write this group now has eleven members, poignantly reminding me of the number of disciples loyal to Christ after
Judas's circumstances ended with him falling away also. As you
will now have gathered from my own story, I know what it's
like to lose my nerve, and you quite probably do too; I don't
judge Judas, because he represents any of us when future fears
overtake the present; spiritually he hit the wall, but I aspire to
remain a follower of Christ throughout my life and am invig-
orated in this aim by the symbolism of this running tribe of
eleven. It is appropriate that the race organisers decided to honour the 'Ever Presents' with guaranteed places in all future London marathons. For me, it's never been about winning; seeing
Mo Farah glide past is thrilling, of course, but the Ever Presents
embody perseverance and a unique bond which comes from
running this particular race. For them, and relative beginners
like me, it's about finishing that race.

I maintain that there is something special about longevity. Today, our relationships are sieved through our pixelated
preferences, rarely mining deep enough to strike weakness,
and often they don't last. Despite pressure from my teenage
children, my family laugh as I steer clear of social media and
the requests of 'friends' because friendship, as I understand it,
takes time and touch. I was struck by it when U2 played their
Joshua Tree anniversary tour and I was in the crowd standing
and applauding. Before those four guys even played a note,
as they walked on stage I was considering the lives these men
have led, the decision to risk everything at the initial stage of
their career, the disagreements and the joys. As they stood side
by side, arm in arm before a gigantic blood-red screen and the

warm recognisable chords began for 'Where the Streets Have No Name', I stood in respect of the loyalty they have come to represent. Perhaps no band will ever endure the demanding world of fame and creativity to this extent again?

Friendships that survive a rock 'n' roll wilderness of thirty years take immense work, and the deliberate investment of our lives in the lives of others; on these terms, I can probably count my friends on two hands, at an honest assessment.

On the 19 February 2019 I was privileged to visit a real 'Ever Present' marathon runner, Bill O'Connor, who took his place at the inaugural event in 1981 at the age of 35. We are both school teachers and hit it off immediately. Originally from New Zealand, Bill stumbled into running after receiving a broken nose on the rugby field and losing confidence, although surprisingly he never made it onto an athletics team at school. Despite his sporting childhood enjoying New Zealand's outdoors, Bill later fell out of shape until a parent of one of the children he taught invited him to his running club, whereupon Bill ran 1 mile before sleeping for fifteen hours. At the age of 19, this was literally Bill's wake-up call to address how unfit he had become, so he took up running. A late starter, you might think, but perhaps there was something within the family (Bill's sister Mary ran the marathon in the summer Olympics of 1984 in Los Angeles, California) which led Bill to compete for various titles and club competitions in New Zealand and shaped him to later become part of the 'Ever Present' group.

Talking to Bill, one appreciates a huge warmth of personality, an insatiable appetite for statistics and a mindset that knows how to win (he showed me silver and gold medals won last weekend in some Veterans' Athletic Club events). Bill's mind is razor sharp all these years later, most likely now enjoyed by those students to whom he teaches mathematics day in, day out. Such investment in young people saw him chosen to carry an Olympic torch in the relay around the UK prior to London 2012, 'probably the slowest 400m I've ever run' he admitted, while wanting to make the most of his moment in the history books. His personality is effervescent; he still runs daily and shows the determination of someone new to the sport. I asked him the secret to sustaining his fitness and he simply told me to 'get out every day'.

Bill was blunt when it came to progress, insisting that 'you get out what you put in'. It's a simple transaction but one which has undoubtedly sustained him through a busy teaching career. When I asked him the benefits of running for fifty-five years he replied, 'It's kept me in teaching,' offsetting the stresses to which we could both relate. This surprised me as I was looking for something a little more reflective, or a pearl of wisdom about running in particular, but Bill generally talked straight to the point. He used to run the 9 miles to work then 9 miles home until around ten years ago, because he simply felt better after running, adding that it helped 'to get away from the world'.

Once again, like so many have concluded, the mental health benefits are obvious when one listens to this inspirational force of a man who defies his years. Perhaps defying years is incorrect; Bill *lives* his years.

The marathon story only began for Bill when members of his club, the Queen's Park Harriers, taunted him enough to persuade him to enter a longer event such as London in 1981. The mile was his main event, but ever up for the challenge, Bill took on twenty-six of them. Although he believes that the real camaraderie lies in the mud, sweat and tears of cross-country running, he took his place in London's road race alongside 6,500 others on a 'perfect morning for running with mist and drizzle, little breeze'. There were few crowds compared with the huge charity fundraising event of today (a change which Bill noted has impacted upon club runners the most because less places are offered to them now), and he recalled after the noise of Tower Bridge they turned right towards the derelict sights off Commercial Road. 'The only high rise sights of that course were St Paul's Cathedral and the Post Office Tower'; I cannot comprehend the great changes to London's skyline that Bill has jogged past as he continues to take his place in an event which has retained its global regard and obvious benefits to tourism, in his opinion.

As we talked, I appreciated that Bill has hit running heights that I will never reach. He has been in the leading pack, breathing alongside the Kenyans, finding the Tempro and sticking to it. He affirmed a belief that I hold after only two compared to his thirty-nine Londons – that 'the real race starts at mile 20' and advised that it's all about being in good shape at this point. Hill running helped him to reach this peak, Primrose Hill to be precise, and once at the top to keep pushing without letting up. Speed work gave him the confidence to run faster marathons. (I could feel myself itching to enter London's next ballot as I made mental notes as we spoke. In the infectious company of someone for whom running is obviously a way of life, being with Bill made me dream of improvement.)

On the unique bond that exists between the 'Ever Presents', Bill said that they keep in touch via emails and occasional get-togethers during the year. He felt 'the burden' of remaining in a club that could never increase, only decrease, commenting that 'we want everyone to stay as long as we can; we're all afraid of dropping out'. I didn't expect this burden admission in the interview, but my own season of church leadership, and close friendship with my 88-year-old mentor and Reader in the Anglican Church, Peter, helped the words to find rest. I empathise with those words; all of us who have pursued vocations have both loved and hated them at times; it hurts, but we love it, we carry a calling walking faithfully towards it, yet sometimes shirking back; I believe Judas represented these extremes. It's where I stand today with so much that goes on in church, but I can neither live with it nor without it. It's Bill and marathons.

Compassionately, the 'Ever Presents' still regard former members (who can no longer take part) as firmly within their elite, which echoes the team dynamic Bill regards highly, maintaining that running is about respect regardless of ability. There is no disgrace in this remaining fraternity, just grace, exactly what I have witnessed from the Parkrun opposite my front door at home in Ashford. As I left Bill's north London home, I thanked him for his inspiration and looked forward to encouraging him along the course next April. I also thanked the unspoken secret to many runners' successes, his wife – who laughed. Without a supportive spouse, I can testify that much of our appetite to succeed would stall. I had been in the presence of a special individual who has found themselves within running history, and all through a bump on the nose.

As I boarded my train back to Kent, I felt deeply grateful for this meeting during which I had learned so much. Counter to the tech surrounding many modern runners, Bill runs with none; he wants to hear the birds. Equally refreshing was the humility of this marathon giant; he did not boast about his achievements, and this too flagged up a character lesson I thought I had dealt with by now. Obviously not. Our interview had been in his lounge with full wooden bookshelves upon which I noticed Shakespeare and Bibles. With a family including a brother serving as a Catholic priest in Pakistan and a sister who had achieved Olympic-standard running, I had wondered whether Bill might represent a combination of them both, like my work here has sought to address, but our flowing conversation never wandered from the running. It is safe to say that I have never come across someone so resolute, so unquestioning that the next run will take place that evening; the next race that following weekend. Yet I believe the very fact he has persisted as an educator of young people at the same time is testament to an investment in the lives of others that could be considered as consistent an example of life lived for other people that you are ever likely to come across; a life of love made possible through running. I was honoured to meet Bill; he suggested we run together sometime – perhaps we will one day.

The 'Ever Presents' no longer post times to make fast runners drool, with the exception of one who still manages to come in under four hours (even with an arm broken in two places after being tripped at 3.5 miles in the 2018 race), something that would take me an immense amount of effort and training. They don't seek to run it quickly, but just complete it, and in faith terms, this is surely what we are all called to do. Finishing the race and keeping the faith is my life goal and means being ever present; present in life, alert, responsive, aware of others' needs, aware of God – remaining one of the eleven.

My discovery of the 'Ever Presents' was an affirmation that God can speak to me through my love of running. Their story felt like my desire for a final canvas, showing evidence that faith, hope and love, and what they mean for me today, were at work in his palette. But practically, what does looking ahead now mean for me as a runner? On a purely physical level, it has always been a challenge to raise my eyes when running. Most runners have a mantra, repeated to assist against fatigue or mental battles that come with the territory. Mine is 'ABC – Arms, Bonce, Cadence'. 'Arms' helps me to relax (I always try to pass my wrists by my hips as if removing a gun from a holster), 'Cadence' refers to my footfall rhythm or frequency of steps, while 'Bonce' is just plain slang and refers to keeping my head up. My son has always commented upon the awkwardness of my style and how I overwork my arms at the elbow, but on hills it works like a dream. 'ABC' stood me in good stead at the Royal Parks Half in 2016 when I received the most memorable compliment from a member of the crowd towards the finish. 'Form' in running refers to our shape, control and overall efficiency of movement – it is best practice to keep your form – and he yelled, 'Good form, Austen!' It was incredibly satisfying to hear from someone who knew about running, and a personal victory for me because I obviously came in looking relaxed while smashing a PB by 20 minutes!

My instinctive metaphor as I shouted 'Yes!' passing underneath the digital clock, was my desire to finish the Christian race and *keep my faith*, as Paul states at the start of this chapter. You see, I want to live and die keeping my form, maintaining the rhythms of prayer, Bible reading, community and love that nurture me towards a more cooperative space for God. I don't want to walk away from these disciplines, these agents of grace, so of course I will keep running for as long as I can.

It sounds appealing, but remaining ever present means that I do not need to know just now. Form has certainly been returning. It's been more than two months since I last ran, halted by the seizures from my haemorrhage. Vulnerability was an unwanted intruder into my invincible athletic world, but through physio I can now do what was impossible when I typed the early pages of this book – walk and write my name with a pen. Endurance running convinced me I would recover and inspires me to finish with form as an ever-present follower of Christ.

In conclusion, I never set out writing to invite you to become a runner. If you have been inspired to become one of the 40,000 athletes who will run the next London, whether you are running 'from' or running 'to', your reason guarded beneath that sponsorship vest, I applaud you. But we don't need more fitness guilt about our frenetic lives, and you may well already be making progress through other disciplines. If you do run already, hence you picked up this book, or have overtaken me dressed as Blackpool Tower in the past, I hope it has provided a quiet reassurance to accompany your many times of isolation as you set out to reach other starting lines. But personally, I hope it has shown how running has been an aid to my faith development and an invitation to me to work through changed perspectives on faith, hope and love. The death of a fairy tale fullness of life, the sudden impact of illness upon hope and the awareness that God is love and I can find him through running, constitute a resurrection of my spiritual and physical life. To run and believe now means to be ever present.

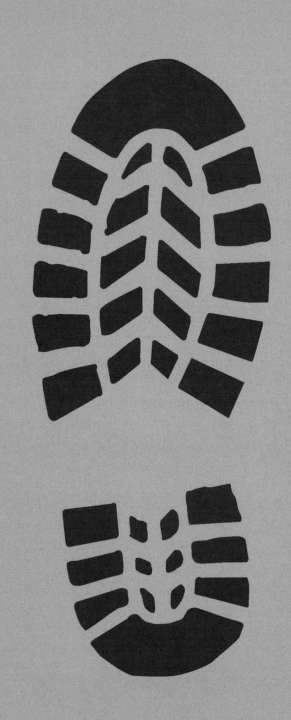

Conclusion (A Final Run)

For I am convinced that neither death nor life, neither
angels nor demons, neither the present nor the future, nor
any powers, neither height nor depth, nor anything else in
all creation, will be able to separate us from the love of God
that is in Christ Jesus our Lord.[1]

I never really knew what these words meant until my experience
of mortality and the necessary place of faith in my ever-fragile
life increased, thanks to my brain cavernoma. But I think I've
edged closer to the enduring love of God in these reflections
upon running. Coming to the end of this book is like turning the corner in front of Buckingham Palace before heading
along The Mall adorned with Union Jack flags and the cheers
of the crowd. The last time I did this, I was hit by a sudden
wave of emotion; a mixture of joy and relief as I passed under
the infamous digital clock, head in hands, wanting to cry, my
challenge completed, before walking through the medals area
where for a brief moment every stranger is a friend and everyone has everything in common; another glimpse of heaven,
perhaps.

Last time I walked through the finisher's enclosure in 2012,
I was recognised by an old friend from a church ten years previously and we made polite conversation, doing our best to

remain composed after the gruelling race we had just endured. I was secretly disappointed that I had not beaten her by running faster. There it was again, the reality of events invading the self-absorbed picture book my imagination had written, as has so often been the case; people interrupting my best-laid plans to go it alone (the very people whose company I crave and make life worth living). Being recognised reminded me again that this human race is not about winning, but about taking part.

I had suspected soon after the start of this project that writing a book about faith and running would be a struggle, and it has certainly left its mark over these months. I began with all the excitement that comes from the arrival of the *Congratulations* magazine landing on the doormat for acceptance into the London Marathon; fervour that knows little of the arduous season ahead. I seemed to have so much to say when I began; my neat ideas of how my book could impact others, how appealing the words would be which would just flow from this well-topped store of years of running and Christian living.

However, as I progressed, there were patches of barrenness, lack of ideas and self-doubt; do I *really* have anything worth saying to anyone? More than that, will they not have thought of it before? Anyway, haven't most people had enough of a Christian religion that has been tried and left wanting in the choir stalls of childhood? Don't preach to runners, they're not like you, and why would runners be interested in faith anyway? They will just discard a book like this and reject you as a weirdo because of it.

But I set out to open up a new road for ordinary people (not just those interested in religion) and if running is a way that you and I can meet honestly side by side and discover something of

God, it's been worth the effort. Father Thomas Keating (who died aged 95 in his home monastery of Spencer, Massachusetts), was known for the practice of 'Centering Prayer' and making the Christian contemplative tradition accessible to people like us. He believed that removing the illusion of an absent or distant God was the purpose of the spiritual journey.[2] I'll risk rejection on the grounds that running has helped me to dismantle this.

The writing process has birthed contrasting insights, helping me to see things of which I'm both proud and ashamed. It's helped me to notice how selfish we distance runners can be; how much we crave our own company. Raising money for charities looks great on paper, but it's not always as altruistic as it seems. Time on the road comes at a cost to those we love, and for me, without the support of my wife and children, I could never do it. So much of this running is actually for my own good – physical and spiritual – so, should I do it? I've never marathon-trained without some self-imposed guilt, but I'll let you decide the greater good of this indulgence.

But a valuable revelation has arisen from my study of the dynamic Christ, especially within the reflections upon Emmaus and Damascus roads and men who experienced blindness such as Bartimaeus. For a life which included restoring physical sight to the blind and metaphorical sight to the Pharisees – the blind religious guides of his own day – one of the first actions upon his arrest and questioning before the Sanhedrin was to be blindfolded by the guards who beat him.[3] The Messiah who gave sight in so many ways was robbed of his own; disorientated and insulted. They took away the very thing he could give to others. It reminds me that amongst all self-doubt when we strive to complete any great dream, or seek to bring positive

change, or improve the lives of others, how often we are robbed
at the point of our strength. You may know this too? You want
to improve others' self-esteem yet none seems more shaky than
your own on the morning you awake to set about such work.
Perhaps this explains my legs of jelly during the first mile of
my most recent marathon and as I near the conclusion to my
writing.

Really, one thing has kept me going, and by now you will
be well aware of my sense that there is a lot more going on
when we run than simply running – a spiritual surgery which
obliterates everything physical. It is this belief that makes me
so evangelical about running, especially because I have spent
much of my life looking for a vocabulary, a way to share my
hunch about the goodness of God through a means that is neither clichéd nor embarrassing, whether to myself or a reader
who doesn't know what to believe in. Jesus has fascinated me
over many miles, his accessibility and his hiddenness, but I
cannot remove myself from the love of God because I have
known that wherever the parasol, his light finds a way through,
another angle where I can feel it. Probably, like you, faith has
changed as I have got older, and I see a less confident Christian
when I look in the mirror. I barely recognise the street preacher
of my early twenties, equipped with the doctrine that would
change the world; a world which was simply black and white.
But it's living with shades of grey that moulds the heart and
challenges the mind, making one more sensitive to the pain of
others once you begin to feel your own pain too, and without
running I would not have been gifted the time to notice this. I
therefore must be loved.

Arnold R. Beisser wrote that 'the reluctance to penetrate into
comprehending the meaning of sports is understandable. We

prefer not to know too much about what we treasure',[4] but I, as author, had a burden to address because these two things, running and faith, seem to exist in a permanent creative unison. Unlike Beisser, the joy, hope and love of running, its captivating pull, *can* be articulated, and I have sought to bring this out through my story where Christian faith provides a language through which I am able to express my treasure. Paul's triangle of faith, hope and love, this tripod upon which these reflections have perched, has given me the tools to get to work. With each angle informing the next, I have learned that Christianity is not exclusively a life of faith at all, but a life of all three, rising and falling, moving centre stage to sing alone before retreating to join the chorus, each at different times. Although the hunger to understand their relationship was initially and selfishly mine from personal experience of faith (puzzlement over fullness of life), hope (through illness) and love (of running), the desire to know God now feels like a gift of grace.

Paramount to Paul's words are, of course, the actions of Jesus, the manner in which he revealed God and the way others have historically become aware of him and still do so today. More a Damascus-road runner, I have seen myself in the injury stories of other runners many times, and we are as bad as each other, often impatient with our inactivity. Honing the skill of awareness when the physical and spiritual breakdowns do occur has been a surprise to me, and I'm still not there all the time.

On that note, I once enjoyed a week's holiday on the Norfolk Broads with three friends who should never have been allowed to board the same barge. We were 'adults' in the loosest sense of the word, occupying ourselves with ejecting smelly trainers into canals and receiving complaints from other river-users via the barge hire company. A high point was our surprise attack, upon some children fishing, with water pistols accompanied by a James Bond soundtrack. From behind their boat upon a muddy riverbank, they stood in silence, digging their wooden oars into the ground and very serenely receiving our attack, oars vertical. Our pistols empty, these wise children then flipped those oars over like the batons of a row of majorettes, pelting our barge (and our faces) with more mud than I had ever seen in a school rugby changing room. Beaten, we dived for cover before making our escape at a breakneck 5 miles per hour along the daffodil-lined canal. Indeed, when life hurls something at us, and we conveniently choose to throw whatever we want at God, we never finally win because he is able to make something of it. This is surely a symptom of his ever-presence. Once impatience has abated, suffering creates space for us all to reflect and an opportunity to become more honest about the past, present and future.

In 2018, I was back working at school for the entire winter, and someone did actually ask me the big 'reformation' question I guessed would come some day, 'Has having a stroke changed you?' I wished that I'd had a neat answer, one phrase that would sum it all up, a movie soundbite of a clearly resounding self-improved man. I stumbled for ideas, acknowledging that I certainly valued health a lot more and appreciated my family around me. But on the inside, I wondered, am I truly changed? And it was in that moment of clutching at straws that I was reminded about the normality of it all: the strokes, the operations, the confusion, the abandoned diary, the fear; experiences that confront so many of us, the *fullest* of life, without which I would not have thought of God in quite the way I now do.

Glimpsing the blue Tempro line, I think I know him more. I have a route, a way that's OK, that is ultimately good, with peaks, troughs and loose ends, but it is consistent because it is divine love. I recommend its quality, his character, love as I understand it, to any honest reader who is prepared to admit that life in all its fullness can be tough and should never be about us, but about an ever-present him.

Although God is, being ever present is not our default way of course. Several years ago, I was reading a bedtime fairy story to my daughter from a book containing one tale for each day of the year. With the poignant innocence of childhood she asked, 'Daddy, how many days of life do I have left?' I was a little stunned. Children have this ability to pull the rug from underneath us, to make us pause when all we are thinking of is completing the washing-up and making sandwiches for work the following morning. I was perhaps not feeling too loving at the time, and cannot even remember my answer, but I never forgot my private thought as I turned out her light and sauntered down the stairs: 'How would I live if I knew the answer to her question?'

Like the many passengers on 11 September 2001 who made phone calls from hijacked planes headed for the Twin Towers, my instinct would be to tell everybody close to me how much I love them. I would probably also want to thank friends for the tremendous role they have played in my life. A remaining luxury would be to tie up any loose ends, relational or practical. And finally, I would want to make peace with God. But in the real world, where suffering enters as an unannounced intruder, time is not always so generous. Instead it marches to a beat we don't wish to hear or work with, fighting it, ignoring it, cursing it. Surely, if my experience has revealed anything, it is that fullness of life is about the very now, the present, fully living, not watching the clock in fear and dread of what might happen tomorrow, or wishing it to be another way. Life in all its fullness is about working with what lies in our hands, the circumstances before us, dancing through them in the partnership God offers, as long as my beating heart allows.

And to achieve that, I would have to go for a final run.

Notes

Introduction: Finding the Blue Line

[1] Rob Parsons, *The Wisdom House* (London: Hodder & Stoughton, 2014), p. 159.

[2] 'A cavernoma may commonly be found in the brain or spinal cord. It is a group of blood vessels resembling a raspberry. They are also referred to as "cavernous angiomas, cerebral cavernous malformation (CCM), or cavernous hemangiomas."' See https://www.nhs.uk › conditions › cavernoma (accessed 25.11.19).

[3] Cavernoma Alliance Annual Forum, 13 June 2015, lecture by Professor Bertalanffy from Hanover.

[4] Bobby Moore, England's World Cup-winning captain of 1966, was my father's cousin and the fund was set up by Bobby's widow, Stephanie Moore, MBE, to fund life-saving bowel cancer research.

[5] James F. Fixx, *The Complete Book of Running* (New York: Random House, 1977), p. 31.

1 At the Third Stroke

[1] 1 Corinthians 13:13.

[2] See John 10:10.

[3] See C.S. Lewis, *The Lion, the Witch and the Wardrobe* (London: Geoffrey Bles, 1950).

[4] See Psalm 46:10.

2 A Running God

[1] Luke 24:12.
[2] Paraphrased: Haruki Murakami, *What I Talk About When I Talk About Running* (London: Vintage Books, 2009), pp. 82–3.
[3] From the Elbow song 'Lippy Kids' on the album *Build a Rocket Boys!* (Polydor). *Build a Rocket Boys!* is the fifth studio album by multi-award-winning band Elbow, entering the album charts at No. 2 on 7 March 2011.
[4] See the hymn by Horatio Spafford (1828–88), 'It is Well With My Soul'.
[5] Galatians 2:2.
[6] Galatians 5:7.
[7] John 20:2.
[8] See Luke 24:10.
[9] John 20:4.
[10] See John 21.
[11] Luke 15:20.
[12] See Kenneth E. Bailey, 'The Pursuing Father', *Christianity Today* (26 Oct. 1998): cover story.
[13] Richard Rohr, 'Christ is Everyman and Everywoman', Daily Meditation, 30 January 2019, Center for Action and Contemplation, cac.org/Christ-is-everyman-and-everywoman-2019-01-30/ (accessed 09.01.20). Copyright © by CAC. Used by permission of CAC. All rights reserved worldwide.

3 Roads to Damascus and Roads to Emmaus

[1] Acts 9:3.
[2] This refers to Edvard Munch, the Norwegian-born expressionist painter, best known for *The Scream* of 1893, whose work visualised anxiety and uncertainty.
[3] This realisation is explained in Malcolm Gladwell's *Outliers: The Story of Success* (New York: Little, Brown and Company, 2008).

4   Figure suggested by Temple in Cliff Temple, *Challenge of the Marathon: A Runner's Guide* (London: Stanley Paul & Co. Ltd., 1981).

5   See Luke 24:13–35.

6   From 1990, Revd Nicky Gumbel, curate at Holy Trinity, Brompton, oversaw the expansion and revision of the Alpha course at the invitation of the Revd Sandy Millar (vicar at that time).

7   John 20:29.

8   A cabin counsellor position is a two-month staffing role whereby five days are spent overseeing the wellbeing of young people bussed in from their communities, often from neighbourhoods where gangs exist. This is followed by two days off, normally spent sightseeing, washing or sleeping until the next camp commences.

9   *The Truman Show*, distributed by Paramount Pictures, 1998, features Jim Carrey as Truman Burbank whose life, arranged for him, is broadcast internationally via hidden cameras.

10 Luke 24:32.

11 Luke 24:29.

12 The Salvation Army Officer's Covenant, 2003 (https://www.salvationist.org/poverty.nsf (accessed 25.11.19).

13 Matthew 4:19.

14 Matthew 22:21.

15 Mark 10:51.

16 Mark 10:52, *The Message*.

17 Luke 18:37.

4 Out of the Fire

1   Selected verses from Psalm 139:7–12.

2   See Revelation 19:7.

3   This event is recorded in Genesis 22:1–19.

4   'Running Up That Hill' is a song by the English singer-songwriter Kate Bush. It was the first single from her album *Hounds of Love*, released in the United Kingdom on 5 August 1985 by EMI.

⁵   The Stig is a character of unknown identity on the British motoring television show *Top Gear*, who sets fast lap times for cars tested.

⁶   Time And Relative Dimensions In Space, Dr Who's means of travel, which seemed bigger inside than outside.

⁷   The Holy Spirit appeared as fire on the Day of Pentecost, as recorded in Acts 2.

⁸   'He Giveth More Grace', Annie Johnson Flint (1866–1932).

⁹   The universal priesthood of all believers is derived from 1 Peter 2:5.

¹⁰ Charles Monroe 'Sparky' Schulz (1922–2000) was the creator of the popular comic strip *Peanuts,* with Charlie Brown as one of its characters.

¹¹ 'Tent-making' was the occupation of the apostle Paul and has become a term to define those who sustain an income through employment alongside church leadership. See Acts 18:3.

¹² See Psalm 139:7.

5 Faith (and Fullness of Life)

¹   John 10:10.

²   See John 10:10.

³   Hope HIV is a charity now known as WeSeeHope, established to change the futures of vulnerable children in Southern and Eastern Africa. See: https://www.weseehope.org.uk/ (accessed 25.11.19).

⁴   Sub 4 means completing the race in under four hours.

⁵   1 Corinthians 15:55,56.

⁶   Peter J. Hodgson, sermon notes on 'Suffering', 2004. Used with permission.

⁷   John 19:30.

⁸   Miracle recorded in Luke 17:11–19.

⁹   'Does God Heal?' 2 Kings 5:1–14, Mark 1:40–45 is a sermon preached in Duke University Chapel on 15 February 2009 by the Revd Dr Samuel Wells. It can be read at https://chapel-archives.oit.duke.edu/documents/sermons/Feb15DoesGodHeal.pdf (accessed 25.11.19).

10 See James Fowler's *Stages of Faith: The Psychology of Human Development and the Quest for Meaning* (San Francisco, CA: Harper & Row, 1981).

11 As above.

12 John 17:3.

13 Oswald Chambers, 18 August, 'Have you ever been expressionless with sorrow?' from *My Utmost for His Highest* (Crewe: Oswald Chambers Publications Association Limited, 1995), p. 237.

6 Blisters

1 Matthew 9:20.

2 Jeremiah 29:11.

3 Dallas Willard, *The Divine Conspiracy: Rediscovering Our Hidden Life in God* (NY: HarperCollins, 1998). Idea from Chapter 1 'Life in the Dark' from HarperCollins eBooks, see https://books.google.co.uk/books/about/The_Divine_Conspiracy.html?id=dQtI3Yg3cdAC&printsec=frontcover&source=kp_read_button&redir_esc=y#v=onepage&q=upside%20down&f=false (accessed 22.11.19).

4 Paraphrased: Malcolm Muggeridge quoting Simone Weil in his article 'Lights in Our Darkness', *The Observer*, 22 September 1968; taken from his book *Jesus Rediscovered* (Garden City, NY: Doubleday & Company Inc., 1969).

5 Jesus cured an epileptic boy (Matthew 17:14–21; Mark 9:14–29; Luke 9:37–43).

6 Romans 8:15.

7 Distributed by IFC Films, 2005.

8 See Ephesians 2:8,9.

9 Quotations from various conversations with Edwin Bartlett at Ashford Parkrun, 2018–19. Used with permission.

10 Ivan Oranksy, 'Ralph S Paffenbarger Jr', *The Lancet* Vol. 370, Iss. 9587, p. 560, 18 Aug 2007. Doi: https://doi.org/10.1016/S0140-6736(07)61280-X.

[11] This track is from The Soul Stirrers' gospel album *The Singles Collection 1950–61* (Acrobat).

7 Hope (Through Illness)

[1] Hebrews 12:1.

[2] Source unknown.

[3] Interview with Ian Richards 29 May 2019, GB race walking Olympian, who incidentally can race walk a Sub 4-hour marathon – quicker than I can run one. All quotes used with permission.

[4] See https://www.nhs.uk/conditions/cavernoma/ (accessed 22.11.19).

[5] See John 1:5.

[6] Reference taken from title of Henry Nouwen's *The Wounded Healer* (London: Darton, Longman & Todd, 1994).

[7] Ken Costa, *God at Work* (W Publishing, an imprint of Thomas Nelson, 2016), p. 133.

[8] A focal seizure (also known as a partial seizure), occurs when there is a disruption of electrical impulses in one part of the brain. A person may be aware that they are experiencing such a seizure.

[9] Elisabeth Kübler-Ross (1926–2004), author of *On Death and Dying* (NY: Macmillan, 1969) where she discussed the five stages of grief outlined here.

[10] See Matthew 2:11.

[11] The *Welcoming Prayer*, as outlined by Phil Fox Rose, 17 October 2013 at http://www.patheos.com/blogs/philfoxrose/2013/10/the-welcoming-prayer/ (accessed 25.11.19).

8 Love

[1] Mark 8:24.

[2] Fixx, *The Complete Book of Running*, p. 37.

[3] As above.

4   Haruki Murakami, *What I Talk About When I Talk About Running* (London: Vintage Books, 2009), p. 16.
5   Mark 8:22–26.
6   1 Corinthians 13:4,5.
7   Fixx, *The Complete Book of Running*, p. 273.
8   Paraphrased: Alan Jamieson, *Chrysalis* (Milton Keynes: Authentic Media, 2007), p. 37.

9 The Spirit of Christmas Past

1   Luke 1:52–53.
2   Charles Dickens, *A Christmas Carol* (London: Chapman & Hall, 1843).
3   Luke 2:1–4.
4   1835–93.
5   Matthew 1:23.
6   The 37 per cent data is from https://www.moneyadviceservice. org.uk/blog/got-a-christmas-present-you-don-t-want-here-s-how-to-return-it (accessed 26.12.14); and 2.4 billion figure from https://www.themoneypages.com/latest-news/2-4-billion-spent-wasted-presents (accessed 15.12.14).
7   The angels declared: 'Glory to God in the highest heaven, and on earth peace to those on whom his favour rests' (Luke 2:14).
8   Luke 1:30.
9   https://www.telegraph.co.uk/news/science/space/12050401/Tim-Peake-launch-British-astronaut-blasts-off-towards-International-Space-Station-live.html (accessed 15.12.15).

10 When Faith and Hope Speak to Each Other

1   Philippians 3:10,11.
2   Philippians 3:14.

3   This charity that exists to support families was created by author and speaker Rob Parsons, OBE. See https://www.careforthefamily .org.uk/ (accessed 22.11.19).

4   The Salvation Army Officer's Covenant, 2003. See https://www .salvationist.org/poverty.nsf (accessed 25.11.19).

5   Jonah fled from God because he did not want to preach to the Ninevites. In Jonah 1:1–3, he found a boat bound for Tarshish from the port of Joppa.

6   Albert Einstein described Christ with these words. https:// bonniewilks.com/2017/01/09/einstein-and-the-luminous-nazarene/ (accessed 22.11.19).

7   Paraphrased: Malcolm Muggeridge quoting Simone Weil in his article 'Lights in Our Darkness' in *The Observer*, 22 September 1968, taken from his book *Jesus Rediscovered*, p. 146.

8   See Matthew 9:12.

9   Paraphrased: 'A Hard Bed to Lie On', in *The Observer*, 20 August 1967, by Malcolm Muggeridge, taken from his book *Jesus Rediscovered*, p. 177.

11   When Hope and Love Speak to Each Other

1   1 Corinthians 9:26, Paul does not live/'run' aimlessly.

2   This paraphrase is based upon the U2 song 'Running to Stand Still' from *The Joshua Tree* album, 1987 (Island Records).

3   This buzz refers to the sense of euphoria coupled with less ability to feel pain and reduced anxiety following aerobic exercise.

4   Michael Heald, article 'The Wall', *Runner's World*, June 2015.

5   Heald, 'The Wall', inmate 'James'.

6   Heald, 'The Wall', inmate Kelley Slayton.

7   Acts 2:47.

8   A 'tempo run' is a training technique involving running at an effort level which means your body produces lactate at the maximum rate your body can clear it.

[9] Temple outlines this process in *The Challenge of the Marathon: A Runner's Guide*, p. 40.

[10] Bill Crotty from Uckfield, East Sussex. Notes taken from Temple, *The Challenge of the Marathon: A Runner's Guide* by Cliff Temple, p. 63.

[11] The late George A. Sheehan (1918–93), once a cardiologist from New Jersey, senior athlete and author of *Running & Being: The Total Experience* (NY: Simon & Schuster, 1978) which became a *New York Times* bestseller. The original quote is in Fixx, *The Complete Book of Running*, p. 249. Source of Sheehan's original quote unknown.

12 When Love and Faith Speak to Each Other

[1] Philippians 3:14.

[2] See Matthew 28:19.

[3] Oswald Chambers, 21 August, 'The ministry of the unnoticed' from *My Utmost for His Highest* (Crewe: Oswald Chambers Publications Association Limited, 1995), p. 240.

13 Ever Present

[1] 2 Timothy 4:7.

[2] Pete Greig, *God on Mute* (Eastbourne: Kingsway Publications, 2007), p. 182.

[3] 1 John 4:16.

[4] 1 Corinthians 13:5.

[5] Attributes of love taken from 1 Corinthians 13:4–7.

[6] Dr Martyn Lloyd-Jones, *Spiritual Depression: Its Causes and Cures*, p. 59.

[7] 1 Corinthians 13:13.

Conclusion (A Final Run)

[1]　Romans 8:38,39.

[2]　From Richard Rohr's email from the Center for Action and Contemplation, 1 November 2018.

[3]　See Mark 14:65.

[4]　Reference to Arnold R. Beisser in 'The Madness in Sports', Fixx, *The Complete Book of Running,* p. 19. Beisser quote is from Arnold R. Beisser, *The Madness in Sports: Psychosocial Observations on Sports* (NY: Appleton-Century-Crofts, 1967).

Infused with Life

*Exploring God's gift of rest in
a world of busyness*

Andy Percey

In a stressful, task-orientated life, we know the importance of rest, but it is too often pushed out of our busy schedules.

Join Andy Percey as he reveals that rest is actually God's good gift to us, provided for us to experience a balance in our lives that isn't just about rest as recovery, but rest as harmony with our Creator and the world he has made.

By learning to practise life-giving rhythms of rest, we can be infused with the very best of the life God freely gives us.

978-1-78893-065-9

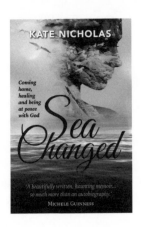

Sea Changed

*Coming home, healing and
being at peace with God*

Kate Nicholas

'I wanted to know how God could love my father yet
allow him to suffer such despair, but no one could give me
a satisfactory answer. God seemed very distant and lacking
in empathy . . . so, in anger, I turned my back and walked
away . . . I knew only one thing, that I had to keep on
travelling until I found the right direction.'

Kate Nicholas's vibrant autobiography allows us to
follow her on her travels in search of faith and truth –
from Aberystwyth to London, through Asia to Australia,
from the US to Africa – and watch her discover a loving,
healing God.

978-1-78078-162-4

A–Z of Prayer

*Building strong foundations for
daily conversations with God*

Matthew Porter

A–Z of Prayer is an accessible introduction that gives practical
guidance on how to develop a meaningful prayer life. It
presents twenty-six aspects of prayer to help you grow in your
relationship with God, explore new devotional styles and
deepen your daily conversations with God.

Each topic has a few pages of introduction and insight, an
action section for reflection and application and a prayer
to help put the action point into practice. There are also
references to allow further study.

978-1-78893-062-8

A-Z of Discipleship

Building strong foundations for a life of following Jesus

Matthew Porter

A–Z of Discipleship is an accessible introduction to the understanding and practice of the Christian faith. It presents twenty-six aspects of discipleship to help you grow in your relationship with God, connect with church and live as a follower of Christ in contemporary culture.

Each topic has a few pages of introduction and insight, an action section for reflection and application and a prayer to help put the action point into practice. There are also references to allow further study.

978-1-78078-456-4

Authentic

We trust you enjoyed reading this book from Authentic. If you want to be informed of any new titles from this author and other releases you can sign up to the Authentic newsletter by scanning below:

Online:
authenticmedia.co.uk

Follow us: